OXFORD
UNIVERSITY PRESS

Great Clarendon Street, Oxford OX2 6DP

Oxford University Press is a department of the University of Oxford.
It furthers the University's objective of excellence in research,
scholarship, and education by publishing worldwide in

Oxford   New York
Auckland   Cape Town   Dar es Salaam   Hong Kong   Karachi
Kuala Lumpur   Madrid   Melbourne   Mexico City   Nairobi
New Delhi   Shanghai   Taipei   Toronto

With offices in
Argentina   Austria   Brazil   Chile   Czech Republic   France   Greece
Guatemala   Hungary   Italy   Japan   Poland   Portugal   Singapore
South Korea   Switzerland   Thailand   Turkey   Ukraine   Vietnam

Oxford is a registered trade mark of Oxford University Press in the UK and in certain other countries

All artwork by Dynamo Design Ltd. Developed with, and English text by, Jane Bingham and White-Thomson Publishing Ltd.
Consultant: David Burnie. Language project manager: Anna Stevenson.

Database right Oxford University Press (maker)

First published 2015

British Library Cataloguing in Publication Data

Data available

ISBN 9780 19 273757 1

Oxford VISUAL DICTIONARY OF ANIMALS

OXFORD

UNIVERSITY PRESS

Contents

Contents

How to use this dictionary

This dictionary is packed with animal words, but it is also an information book. This means that you can find out about the natural world while you are learning new words! The dictionary is divided into nine main sections. Each section is colour coded and starts with a dramatic opening scene, followed by a general introduction to the topic. You can look at the top of the page to identify a section (such as Rainforest creatures or Animals of the Polar Regions). Then you can check the side panel on each page to find its specific subject.

How do I use the dictionary?

Words are introduced through pictures, scenes and labelled diagrams. This makes it easy to find the word you need – and discover more along the way.

Top bar identifies the topic section.

Feature panels give more in-depth vocabulary.

Captions tell you more about certain animals.

Side bar identifies the subject.

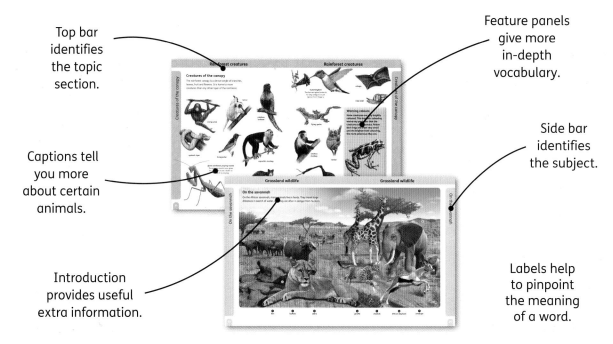

Introduction provides useful extra information.

Labels help to pinpoint the meaning of a word.

How do I find a word?

There are several ways to search for a word. You can look through the topics on the Contents page. The colour coding on each section will help you find the different topic sections. You can also use the Index at the back of the book. There are many hundreds of animal names to find, as well as other words related to animal life.

How is it organized?

The dictionary begins with an overview of animal life and animal behaviour, followed by a description of the main animal groups. Then there are six sections of animal habitats which introduce animals according to where they live.

There are some animals which live all over the world and these are included in the widespread creatures pages. At the back of the book is a vocabulary builder to give you lots more words to use when talking about animals.

pages 10-13
Animal life and behaviour

This section introduces the enormous range of animal life on Earth. It looks at the ways different creatures move, eat and use their senses. It also covers animal behaviour, such as finding a mate, migration and hibernation. Creatures of all types and from all over the world are featured in these pages.

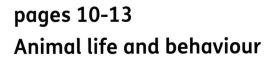

pages 14-27
All kinds of animals

There are six main animal groups:

- mammals
- amphibians
- birds
- fish and other sea creatures
- reptiles
- insects and minibeasts

In this section you will discover the unique features of each group. Labelled images provide a visual guide to the different parts of the animals' anatomy. Information panels focus on different aspects of animal development and behaviour.

pages 28-105

Animal habitats

Next you will discover eight different animal habitats or biomes.

The eight habitats are:

- rainforests
- forests and woodlands
- mountains
- grasslands
- rivers, lakes and wetlands
- deserts
- ocean zones
- polar regions

Each habitat is introduced by a stunning scene, giving you the sense that you are entering a new environment. This opening scene is followed by an introduction to the habitat and the animals that live in it. Maps provide a visual guide to where each habitat can be found around the world, and there is information on the different living conditions within each wildlife habitat. Captions provide extra information about the special features or behaviour of some of the animals.

You will discover new and familiar animals, birds and insects in these dramatically different habitats.

pages 106-109

Widespread creatures and birds

Some types of creatures, such as insects and birds, live in a wide variety of habitats across the world. These pages introduce some of the different creatures that you might encounter anywhere in the world.

How to use this dictionary

Vocabulary builder

pages 110-113
Animal words

A section on words used specially for animals. There are lists of words for young animals, for groups of animals, and for the sounds that animals make. Take a look at these pages to learn some fun new words!

pages 114-116
Animal word origins

A section giving the background for many animal names from aardvark to wildebeest and the way that animal words are used in our daily speech.

page 117
Animal idioms

Idioms are phrases or groups of words which have a special meaning which is not clear from the individual words. This guide gives you some of the idioms we use featuring the animals in this dictionary.

pages 118-119
Animal detective quiz

A fun quiz that offers you the chance to test your animal knowledge.
All the answers can be found within the pages of this dictionary
so have a close look to see if you can get them all right!
For the Answers, look on P126-127.

Animal life

There are millions of species of animals on Earth and they come in an amazing range of shapes and sizes! Some tiny creatures can only be seen with the help of a microscope. The largest animal on Earth is the Blue Whale.

Vertebrates and invertebrates

Animals can be vertebrates or invertebrates. Vertebrates have a spine (or backbone). Invertebrates do not have a spine. Some invertebrates have soft bodies, and some have a hard outer covering.

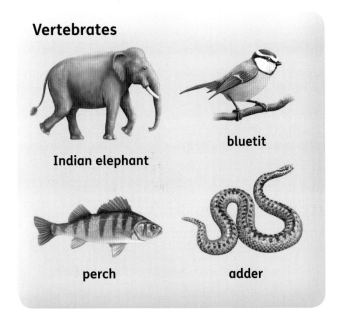

Vertebrates

Indian elephant

bluetit

perch

adder

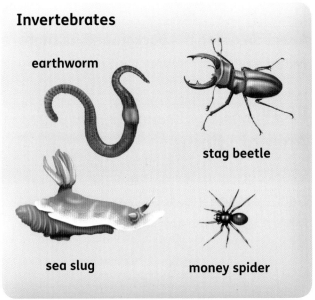

Invertebrates

earthworm

stag beetle

sea slug

money spider

Moving and eating

Animals are different from other living things, such as plants and fungi, because they are more mobile and they survive by eating other life forms. They can be divided into three groups, according to what they eat. Carnivores eat meat. Herbivores eat plants. Omnivores eat meat and plants.

Sheep graze on grass. They are herbivores.

Tigers hunt and kill their prey. They are carnivores.

Animal life

Parasites

Parasites feed off the body of another animal. The animal that a parasite feeds off is known as the 'host'.

Tapeworms live inside the guts of other animals.

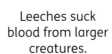

Leeches suck blood from larger creatures.

Fleas live in the coats of mammals and birds.

Animal senses

Animals use their senses of sight, hearing, smell and touch to help them to find their food and to stay safe. Different animals rely on different senses.

Owls have large eyes that let in a lot of light so they can hunt at night.

Mice use their whiskers to check if they can fit through a space.

A wolf's powerful sense of smell allows it to track an animal's scent.

Rabbits use their long, flexible ears to listen out for danger from all sides.

Animal behaviour

Scientists who study animals are called zoologists. They observe animals very closely and study their behaviour. These two pages cover a range of animal behaviour: courtship, fighting, migration and hibernation.

Courtship

Most creatures need to find a mate in order to create new life. Males use a wide range of courtship behaviour to help them win a mate. Courtship rituals are designed to attract the attention of a female and to show that a male is better than his rivals.

The bowerbird collects colourful objects.

The fiddler crab waves its enormous claw.

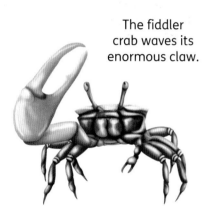

Tree frogs make repeated loud croaks.

The bird of paradise displays its plumage.

Fighting

Males often have to fight off other rivals before they can win their mate. This behaviour means the strongest males win the best mates.

Rattlesnakes try to push each other to the ground.

Stags lock antlers to fight.

Animal behaviour

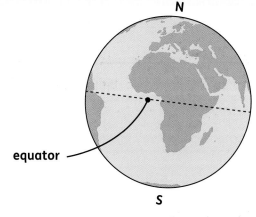

Migration

Some animals make very long journeys to breed or find food. This is called migration. Many migrating creatures make the same journey each year. They always travel around the same time of the year.

equator

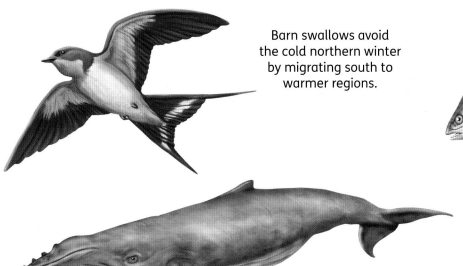

Barn swallows avoid the cold northern winter by migrating south to warmer regions.

Atlantic salmon are born in rivers, migrate to the ocean, and then return to the same river to breed.

Humpback whales give birth near the equator, but their main feeding grounds are in the polar seas.

Hibernation

In the cold winter months some animals hibernate. They sink into a very deep sleep and all their body functions slow down. Before they start to hibernate, some animals consume a large amount of food. This helps to keep them strong while they are hibernating.

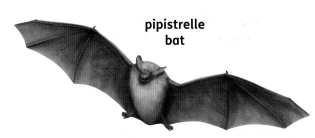

pipistrelle bat

hamster

box turtle

bumblebee

An amazing range of creatures lives on Earth. This section introduces the main animal groups: mammals; birds; reptiles; amphibians; fish and other sea creatures; and insects and minibeasts.

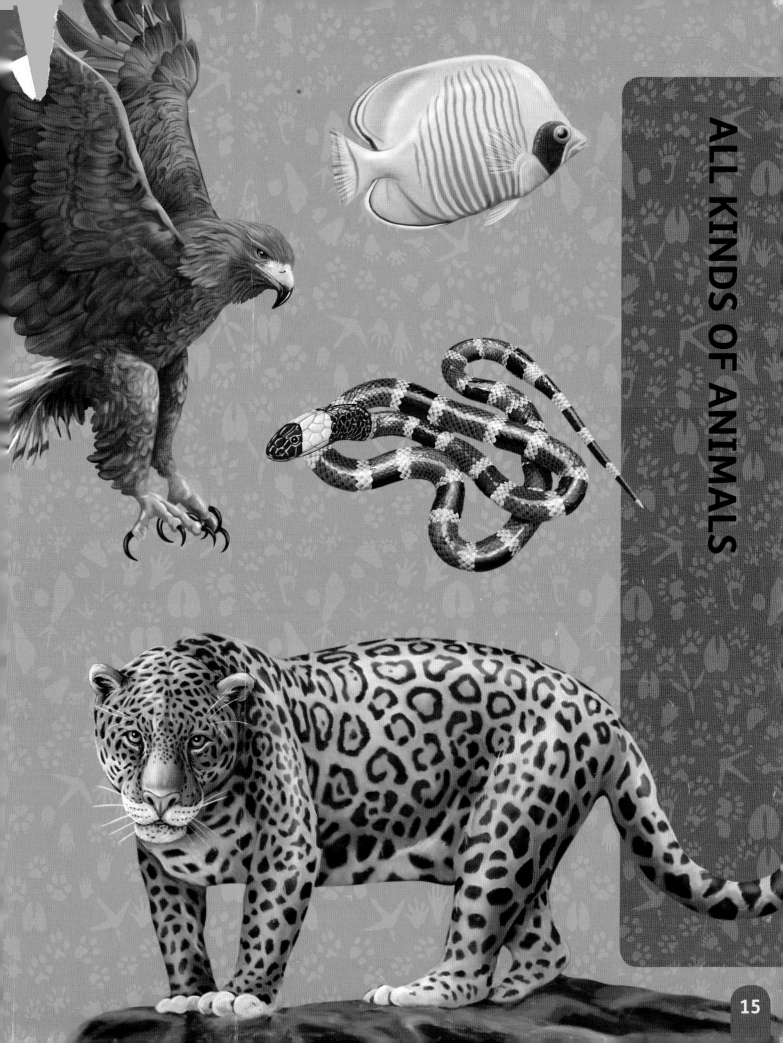

Mammals

Mammals range in size from tiny dormice to enormous elephants. They include bats and whales and, of course, human beings! All mammals are warm-blooded (which means their bodies always stay warm). They all have fur, bristles or body hair and all mammal mothers produce milk to feed their young.

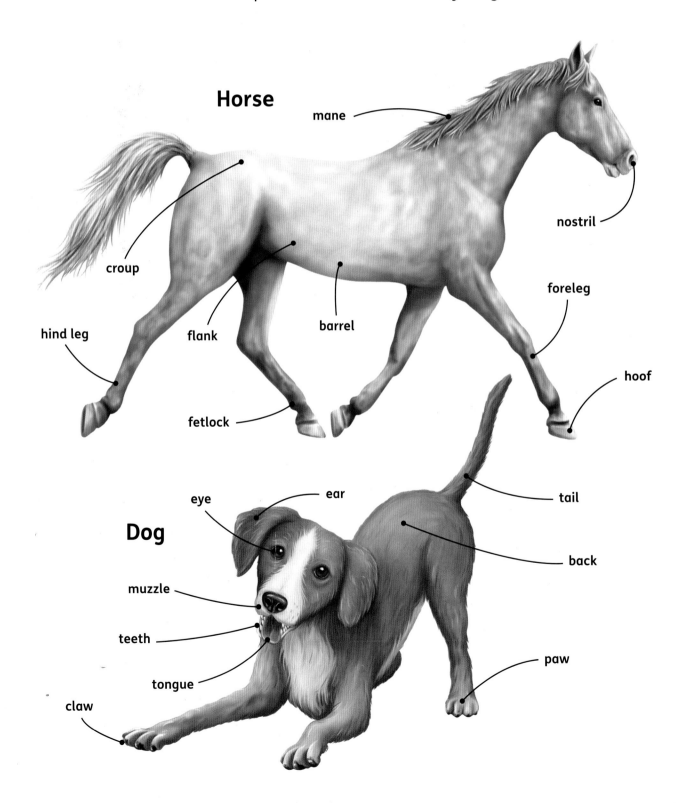

Horse

mane

nostril

croup

foreleg

hind leg

flank

barrel

hoof

fetlock

Dog

eye

ear

tail

muzzle

back

teeth

tongue

paw

claw

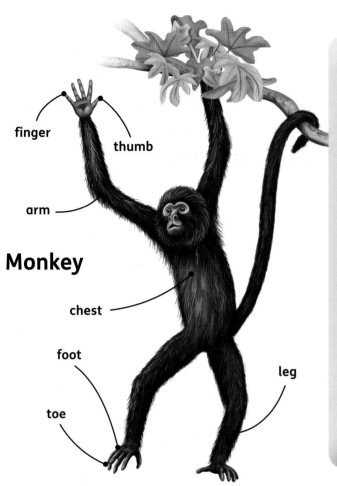

Monkey

finger

thumb

arm

chest

foot

toe

leg

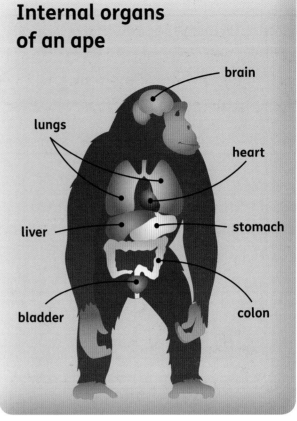

Internal organs of an ape

brain

lungs

heart

liver

stomach

bladder

colon

Marsupials

Marsupials belong to a small group of mammals that are mainly found in Australia. The mothers carry their babies in a pouch until the babies are old enough to survive on their own.

Marsupials living in Australia include kangaroos, wallabies and wombats. A few species of marsupials are found in North and South America. They include opossums and shrew opposums.

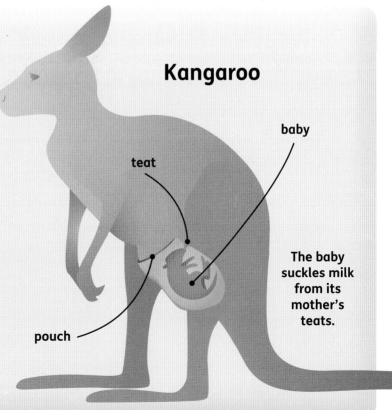

Kangaroo

baby

teat

pouch

The baby suckles milk from its mother's teats.

Birds

Birds are warm-blooded and covered with feathers. All birds lay eggs and most of them can fly, although there are a few large flightless birds, such as the ostrich and the penguin. Many birds perch in trees and spend most of their time in the air. Some birds can swim and live mainly on water.

wingtip

beak

wing

Eagle

tail

talons

Feathers

Many birds have three types of feather. Each type of feather has a different shape and each has its own important function.

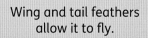

Body feathers give the bird a streamlined shape.

Down feathers keep the bird's body warm.

Wing and tail feathers allow it to fly.

Different bills

Bills are sometimes called beaks. They have a range of different shapes that are suited to different ways of feeding.

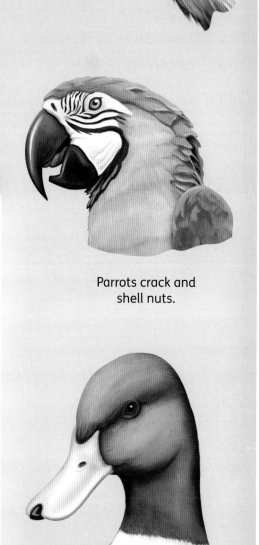

Waders grab fish underwater.

Birds of prey tear up their food.

Parrots crack and shell nuts.

Goose

neck

bill

breast

webbed feet

Ducks scoop up food from the water's surface.

Reptiles

Reptiles have a dry, tough skin that is covered with scales. All reptiles are cold-blooded, so they need to bask in the sun to warm up. Reptiles include crocodiles, lizards, turtles and snakes.

Crocodile

nostril

snout

scaly skin

jaw

claws

Turtle

flipper

shell

underbelly

Camouflage

Many animals use camouflage to help them blend in with their surroundings. Their colouring makes them hard for hunters to spot.

Burmese python

Chinese water dragon lizard

Hermann's tortoise

Snake

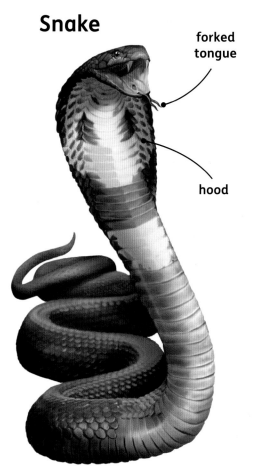

forked tongue

hood

Venom

Some snakes and lizards inject a poison called venom into their prey. They use their fangs to puncture a victim's skin and then inject their poison. Venom can paralyse or even kill a victim.

Viper

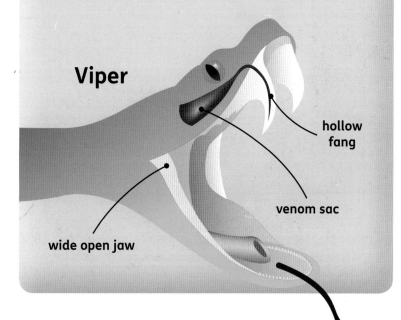

hollow fang

venom sac

wide open jaw

21

Amphibians

Amphibians have smooth skin, with no scales or hair. They are cold-blooded. They usually hatch and develop in water, but then spend most of their adult lives on land. Frogs, toads, salamanders and newts are all amphibians. There are also some amphibians that look like large worms.

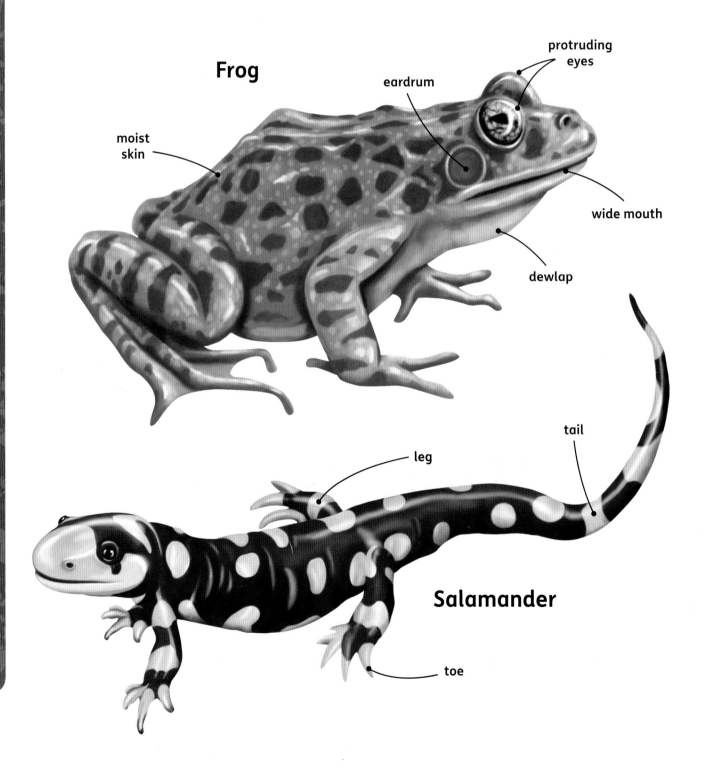

Frog

protruding eyes

eardrum

moist skin

wide mouth

dewlap

tail

leg

Salamander

toe

Lifecycle of a frog

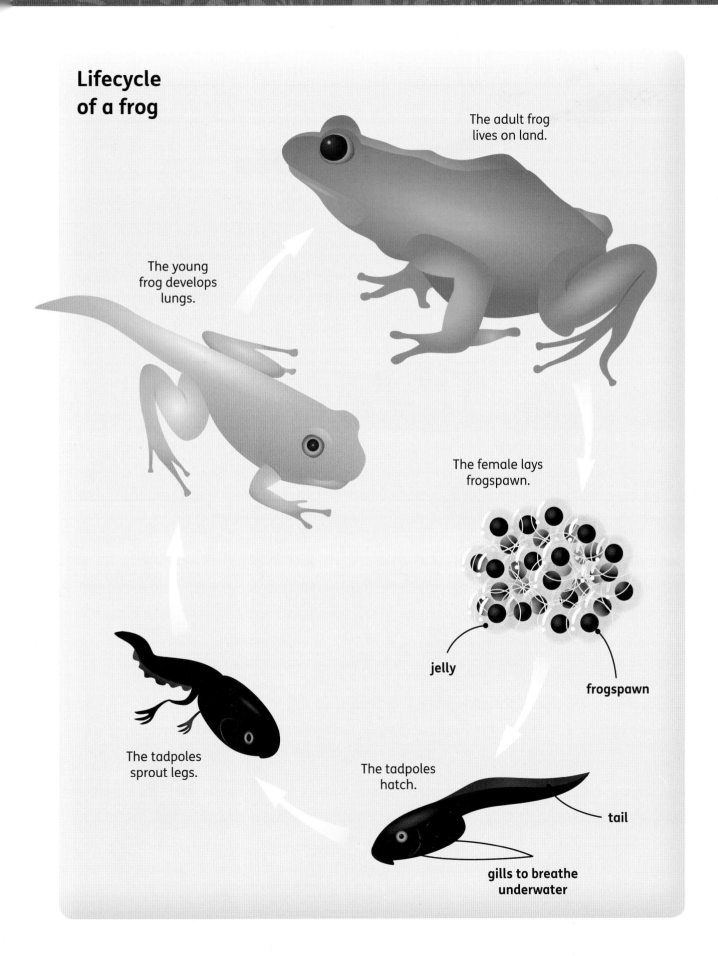

The adult frog lives on land.

The young frog develops lungs.

The female lays frogspawn.

jelly

frogspawn

The tadpoles sprout legs.

The tadpoles hatch.

tail

gills to breathe underwater

Fish and other sea creatures

Fish are creatures with backbones that are specially adapted to live underwater. Other sea creatures include sponges, worms, jellyfish, starfish, squid and lobsters. Many sea creatures are microscopic – they can only be seen with the help of a microscope.

Fish

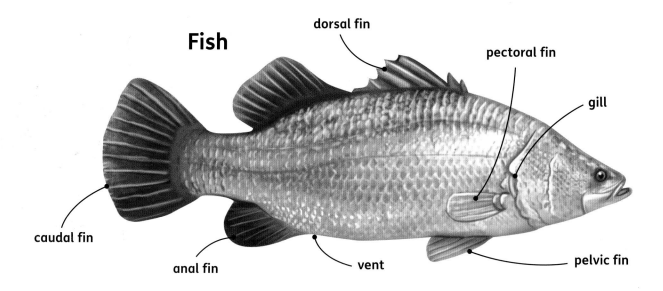

dorsal fin

pectoral fin

gill

caudal fin

anal fin

vent

pelvic fin

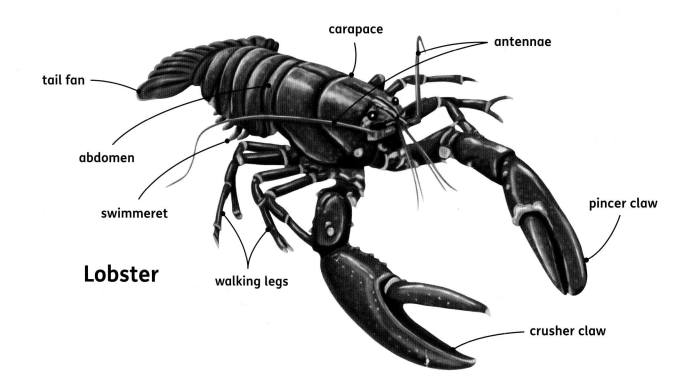

carapace

antennae

tail fan

abdomen

swimmeret

pincer claw

Lobster

walking legs

crusher claw

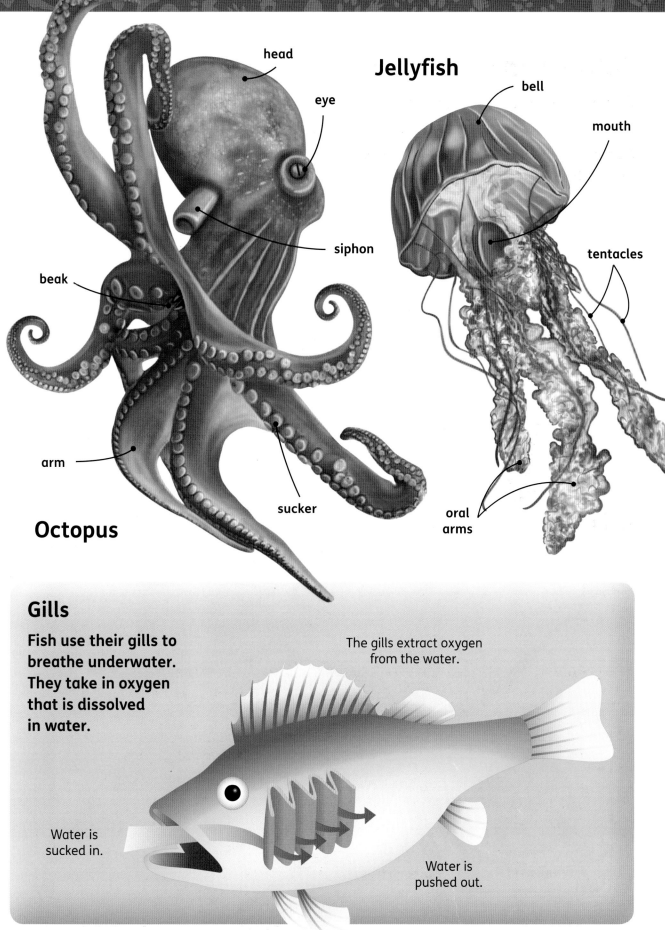

head

eye

Jellyfish

bell

mouth

siphon

beak

tentacles

oral arms

sucker

arm

Octopus

Gills

Fish use their gills to breathe underwater. They take in oxygen that is dissolved in water.

The gills extract oxygen from the water.

Water is sucked in.

Water is pushed out.

Insects and minibeasts

Insects have bodies with three parts: the head, the thorax and the abdomen. All insects have six legs, and some have wings. Insects include beetles, butterflies and bees. Minibeasts are small creatures without a backbone. They include spiders, centipedes and woodlice.

Insects make up the biggest group of living creatures. There are over 900 thousand different species of insects, and eight out of ten of all the world's creatures are insects.

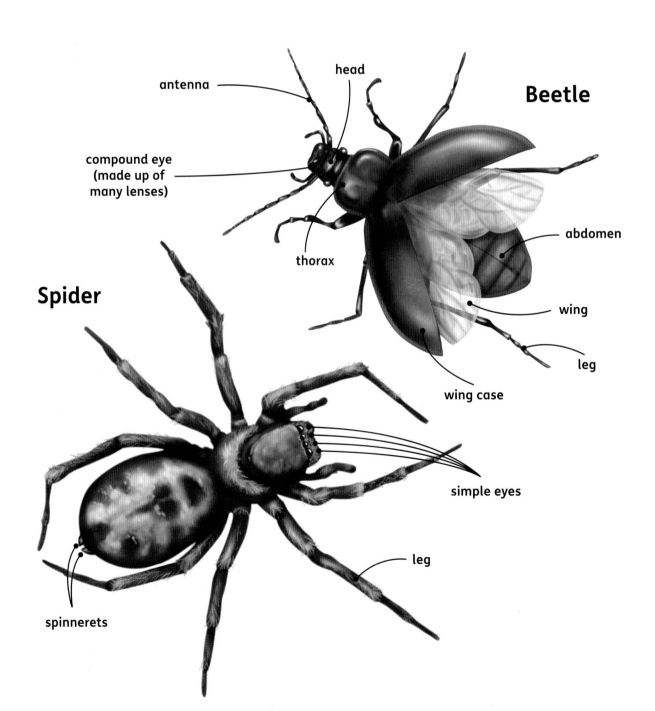

Beetle

antenna

head

compound eye (made up of many lenses)

thorax

abdomen

wing

leg

wing case

Spider

simple eyes

leg

spinnerets

Honey bee

The honey bee collects nectar from inside flowers and spreads pollen from one flower to another.

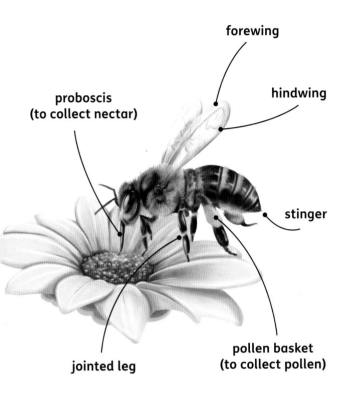

forewing

hindwing

proboscis
(to collect nectar)

stinger

jointed leg

pollen basket
(to collect pollen)

Beehives

A beehive is home to a colony of bees. The colony is made up of a single queen bee, hundreds of drones and thousands of workers.

queen
The queen lays eggs to produce more bees.

drone
Drones mate with the queen to start new hives.

worker
Workers look after the young and make honey.

Lifecycle of a butterfly

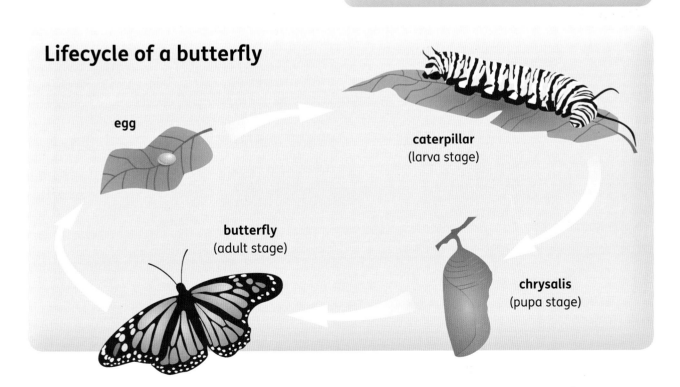

egg

caterpillar
(larva stage)

butterfly
(adult stage)

chrysalis
(pupa stage)

Inside the rainforest it is hot and steamy and very noisy. There are parrots screeching, tree frogs croaking, insects buzzing, monkeys howling and even tigers growling...

Rainforest creatures

Rainforest habitats

Most rainforests are tropical. They grow close to the equator, where it is hot and rainy all year round. Temperate rainforests grow in cooler parts of the world. They are further from the equator, and are often found along the coast. Rainforests are home to an astonishing range of species. The world's largest rainforest is the Amazon in South America. One in ten of all the world's known species live in the Amazon rainforest.

Rainforest layers

Rainforests have four main layers. Each one is home to different animals, although some creatures move between the layers.

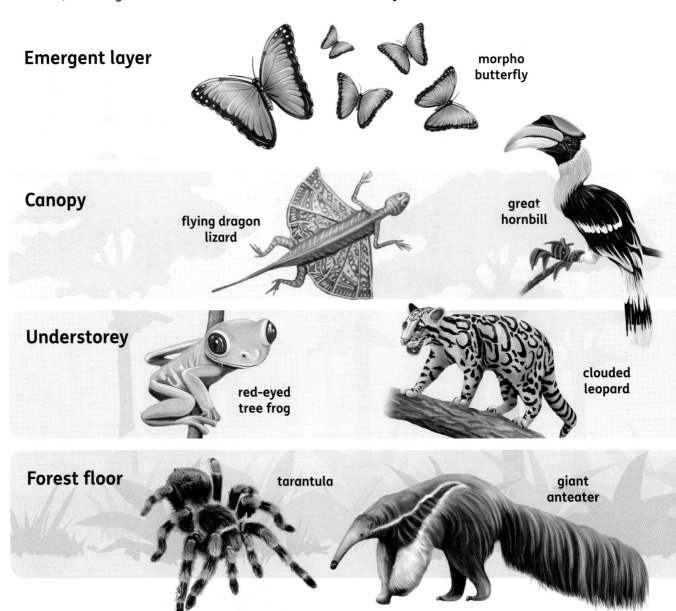

Emergent layer — morpho butterfly

Canopy — flying dragon lizard, great hornbill

Understorey — red-eyed tree frog, clouded leopard

Forest floor — tarantula, giant anteater

Rainforest creatures

Major rainforest regions

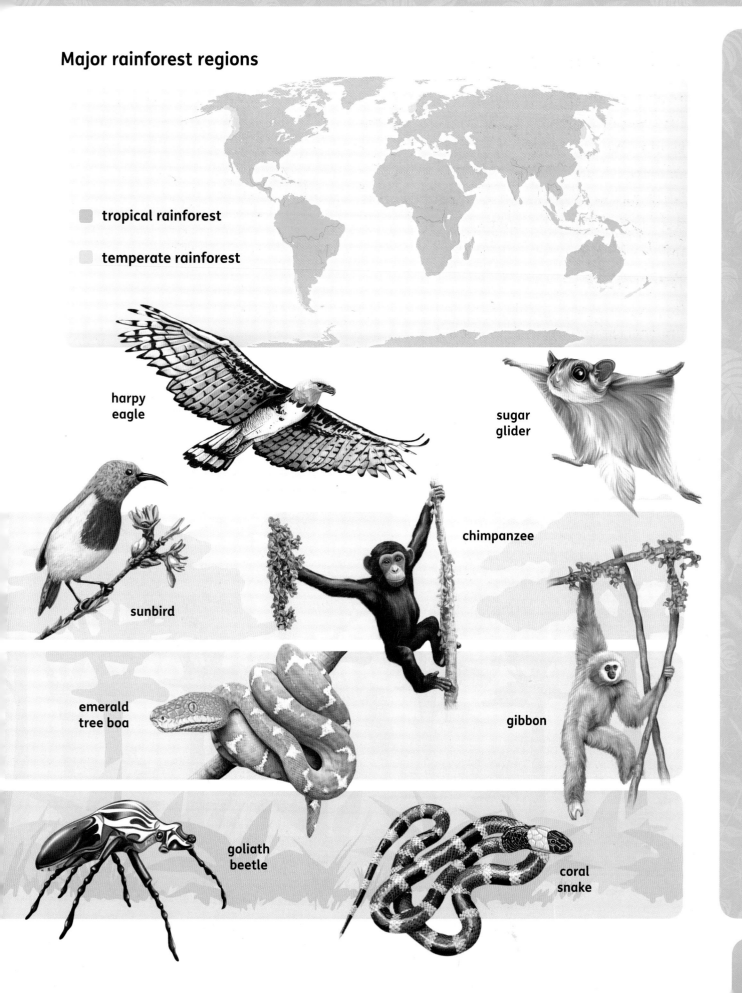

tropical rainforest

temperate rainforest

harpy eagle

sugar glider

sunbird

chimpanzee

emerald tree boa

gibbon

goliath beetle

coral snake

Life on the rainforest floor *(vertical text, left margin)*

Life on the rainforest floor

Very little light reaches the forest floor. Insects and reptiles live among leaves and vines, while mammals and flightless birds weave their way through the tree trunks. Some of the creatures that prowl the forest floor are very large. Elephants, gorillas and tigers all live in the rainforest.

There are also some giant insects, such as the Hercules beetle, which measures around 15cm (6 inches) and can lift eight times its own weight!

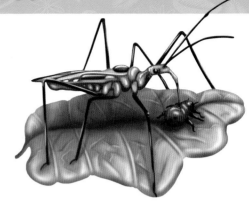

assassin bug
Assassin bugs inject their prey with a deadly saliva that turns body contents to liquid.

tapir

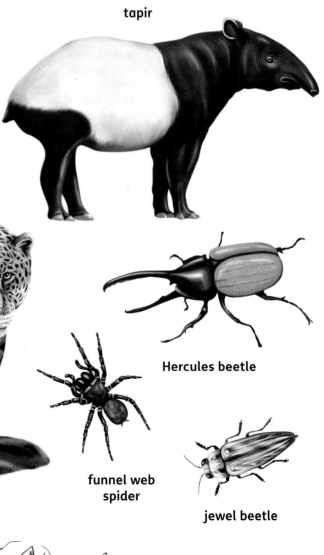

jaguar
Jaguars prowl through the undergrowth and also climb up into the understorey.

Hercules beetle

funnel web spider

jewel beetle

army ants

Rainforest creatures

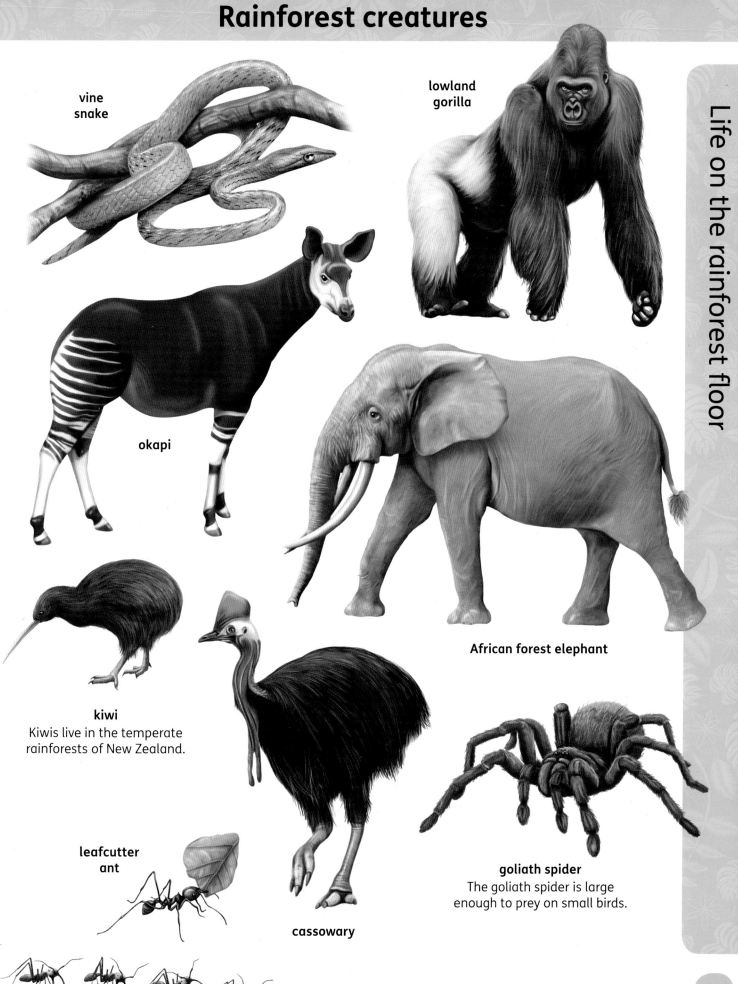

vine
snake

lowland
gorilla

okapi

African forest elephant

kiwi
Kiwis live in the temperate
rainforests of New Zealand.

leafcutter
ant

cassowary

goliath spider
The goliath spider is large
enough to prey on small birds.

Creatures of the canopy

Creatures of the canopy

The rainforest canopy is a dense tangle of branches, leaves, fruit and flowers. It is home to more creatures than any other layer of the rainforest.

lemur

rainbow lorikeet

orang-utan

eyelash viper

honeyeater

capuchin monkey

giant rainforest praying mantis
The praying mantis was given its name because it looks as though it is praying.

tree kangaroo

Rainforest creatures

colugo

hummingbird
The hummingbird extends its long tongue to suck nectar from flowers.

tree snail

flying gecko

colobus monkey

tarsier

Warning colours
Some creatures are very brightly coloured. This dramatic colouring warns any predators that the creatures are poisonous. Poison dart frogs are often very small and the brighter their colouring, the more poisonous they are.

poison dart frogs
Poison dart frogs were given their name because the rainforest people dipped their hunting darts in the frogs' poison.

giraffe weevil
The giraffe weevil uses its very long neck to help it fight.

In the Amazon rainforest

In the Amazon rainforest

The Amazon rainforest contains millions of animal species. The creatures shown here live in the Amazon canopy. Most canopy-dwellers are vegetarian, but some prey on small creatures.

① scarlet macaw

② woolly monkey

③ Amazon parrot

④ morpho butterfly

⑤ green iguana

⑥ three-toed sloth
Sloths sleep for up to 20 hours a day.

⑦ spider monkey

⑧ coatimundi

⑨ keel-billed toucan

⑩ pygmy marmoset

⑪ howler monkey
Howler monkeys are known for the loud howls they make at the beginning and end of the day.

⑫ poion dart frog

Beneath the shelter of the trees are countless creatures. Animals, birds and insects live on the forest floor or make their homes in tree trunks and branches...

Forest habitats

There are two main types of forest in the cooler parts of the world. Deciduous forests have trees that shed their leaves in winter. They are sometimes known as broadleaf forests. Evergreen forests have trees that stay green all year round. They are sometimes called evergreen forests.

Forest habitats are in danger all over the world. As the world population grows, people settle in regions that were once covered with forest, and trees are cut down for timber and fuel.

Deciduous forests and woodlands

Deciduous forests usually grow in regions where there is plenty of rain. There are many deciduous forests in Europe and eastern America.

brimstone butterfly

garden snail

woodpecker

fallow deer

chipmunk

Major regions of deciduous and evergreen forest

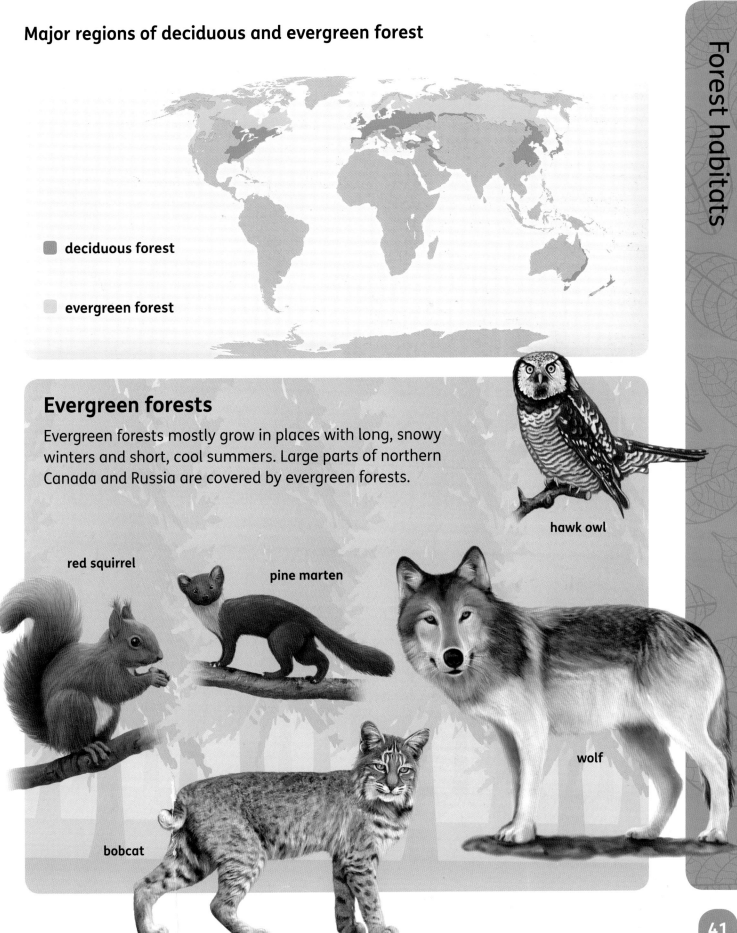

deciduous forest

evergreen forest

Evergreen forests

Evergreen forests mostly grow in places with long, snowy winters and short, cool summers. Large parts of northern Canada and Russia are covered by evergreen forests.

hawk owl

red squirrel

pine marten

wolf

bobcat

Deciduous forest creatures

Many animals in deciduous forests feed on nuts, berries and insects. When the trees lose their leaves, most mammals hibernate. They wake up again when spring arrives and there is plenty of food to eat.

nightingale
The nightingale is famous for its beautiful song.

wild turkey
Wild turkeys roam free in some American woodlands.

red deer
Some creatures, like red deer and grey squirrels, live in both deciduous and evergreen forests.

raccoon

Forest and woodland wildlife

weasel

wood warbler

wood pigeon

grey squirrel

Tasmanian devil
The Tasmanian devil is only found in Tasmania, Australia.

red fox

tawny owl
The tawny owl is also known as the brown owl.

Life on a woodland floor

This scene shows creatures in a deciduous woodland. Some dig burrows in the earth. Some live in rotting leaf mould on the forest floor. The minibeasts shown under the microscope are all found in the leaf mould of a deciduous wood.

1 stoat

2 mole

3 badger

4 dormouse

5 shrew

6 hedgehog
Hedgehogs are protected by spiny quills.

Creatures in the leaf mould

7 woodlouse

8 centipede

9 earthworm

10 millipede

Evergreen forest wildlife

Creatures in an evergreen forest need to cope with freezing, snowy winters. Some mammals grow thick coats and some hibernate. Birds usually migrate south for the winter. They return to the forests in the spring, when the weather warms up and they can find enough food to eat.

Steller's jay

black bear

skunk
If they are attacked, skunks release a very strong smelling spray.

lynx

Forest and woodland wildlife

treecreeper

great grey owl
Owls are nocturnal, so they usually hunt at night.

moose
The male moose uses its giant antlers to fight other males.

polecat

wolverine

porcupine

Eagles soar among the high mountains. Snow leopards stalk their prey on rocky peaks, and pandas live in forests on the lower slopes...

MOUNTAIN ANIMALS

Mountains habitats

Mountains are found in all the world's continents. The Andes, the Rockies, the Himalayas and the Alps are all major mountain ranges. Some very high mountain peaks are covered with snow all year round. Only a few species can survive in these harsh conditions. Some mountains in tropical regions have dense rainforests on their lower slopes. Pandas and gorillas are found in these mountain forests.

Upper and lower slopes

Most mountains provide two different habitats. The steep upper slopes are bare and rocky and often blanketed with snow. The gentle lower slopes are generally covered with trees.

Upper slopes

mountain goat

bearded vulture

Lower slopes

vicuña

red panda

Mountain animals

Major mountain ranges

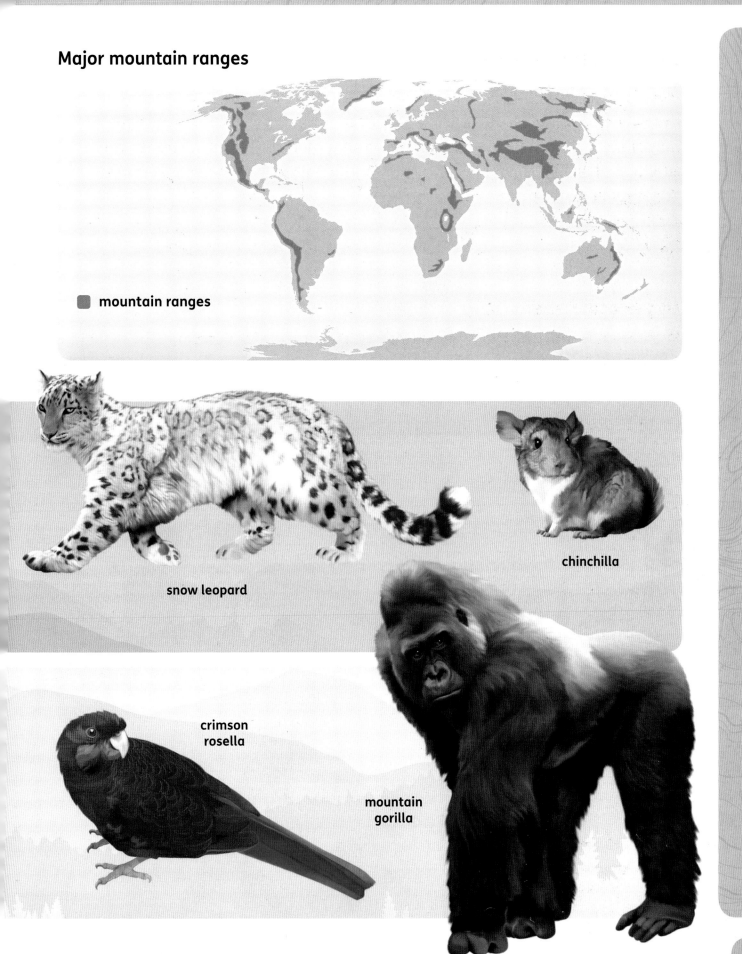

mountain ranges

snow leopard

chinchilla

crimson rosella

mountain gorilla

Life in the mountains

Finding food and shelter on the mountain tops is hard, so animals like the chamois and cougar move between the upper and lower slopes. Most other creatures stay in the highland forests. The giant panda lives only in mountain forests as its lowland habitat has been destroyed. It feeds on the bamboo plants that grow in the forests.

chamois

cougar
Puma is another name for cougar.

Mountain birds

Many birds of prey hunt on mountain slopes where they can easily spot their prey. Their large, powerful wings allow them to soar to very high places. But birds of prey are not only found in mountain regions. They are also at home in other habitats, such as open grasslands, where they can view their prey.

red kite

common buzzard

peregrine falcon

golden eagle

Mountain animals

Domesticated creatures

Some mountain creatures have been domesticated by humans. They have been bred as working animals, pets and farm animals. Yaks and llamas are used for carrying loads, and for their wool and meat. Alpacas are bred for their very fine wool.

llama

yak

alpaca

cavy
Cavies are the wild ancestors of guinea pigs.

giant panda
Giant pandas are in danger of becoming extinct.

ibex

On the wide open grasslands, herds of antelope graze peacefully. Meanwhile, deadly hunters lie in wait...

GRASSLAND WILDLIFE

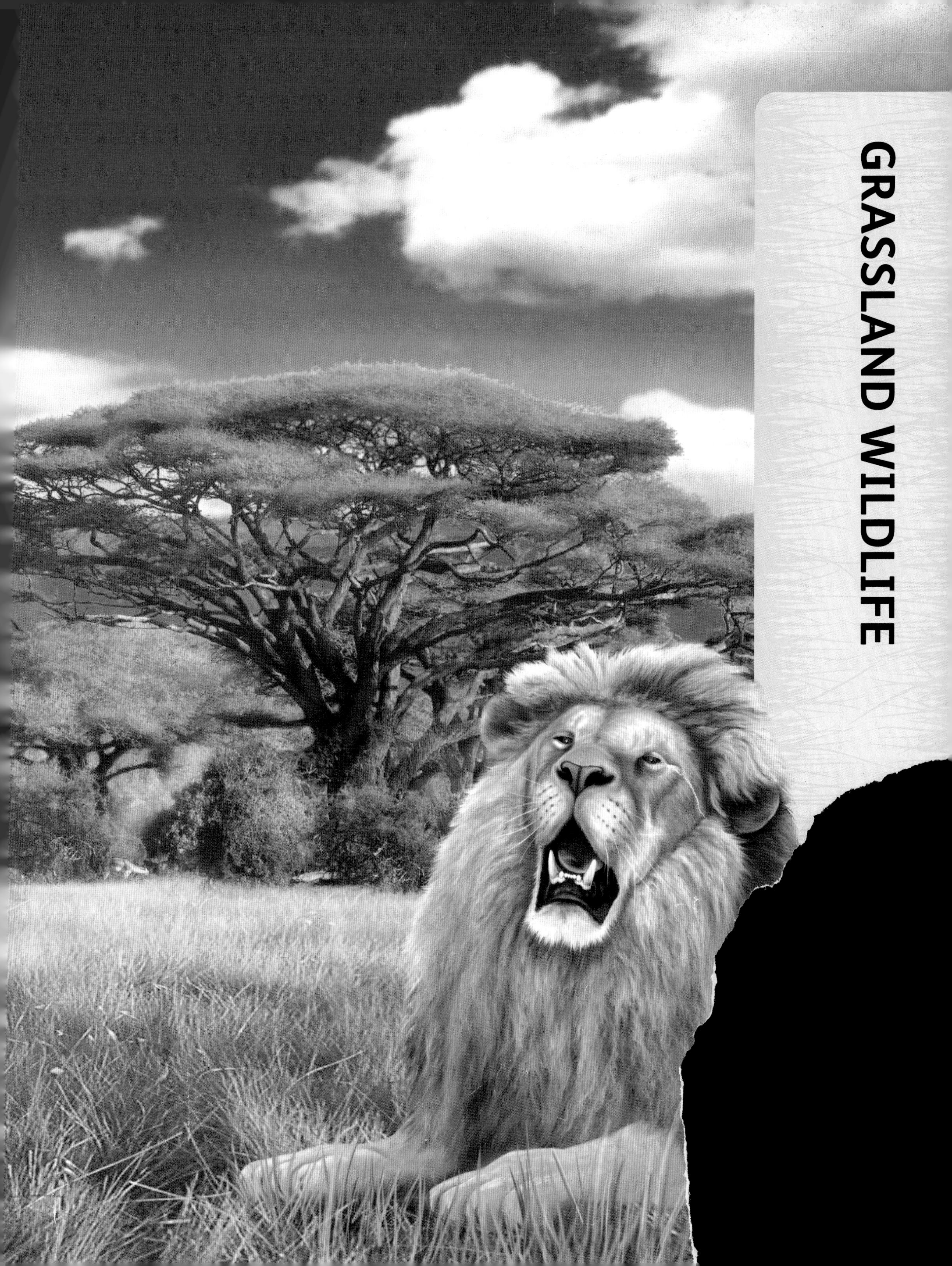

Grassland habitats

Grasslands are large stretches of ground covered by wild grasses and shrubs. They are found in both hot and cold regions, and are given different names in different parts of the world.

Hot, dry grasslands

Some hot, dry grasslands are called savannahs. There are savannahs in Africa, Asia and South America. The South American grasslands are sometimes known as the Pampas.

ostrich

gazelle

Cooler grasslands

The grasslands of North America are called the Prairies. They have hot summers and cold, wet winters. There are also cool grasslands in northern Asia. They are known as the Steppes.

bison

jackrabbit

Grassland wildlife

Major grassland regions

grassland

Bush and scrub

Many parts of Australia are covered with grasses and scrub. These hot, dry regions are known as the bush. Eucalyptus trees, or gum trees, also grow in many parts of the Australian bush.

wombat

goanna

common adder

pheasant

Moorlands

Moors are found in cool regions, with plenty of rain. They have low bushes and shrubs which provide good cover for wildlife. In winter, they are often covered in snow. In the warmer months, they can be boggy.

On the savannah

On the African savannah, many animals live in herds. They travel large distances in search of water, and they are often in danger from hunters.

| **1**
lion | **2**
buffalo | **3**
zebra |

Grassland wildlife

4 giraffe

5 cheetah

6 African elephant

7 antelope

More savannah creatures

Many animals of the savannah escape from predators by running very fast. Some burrow underground to stay safe. The rhinoceros and the armadillo are protected from attack by their tough outer covering.

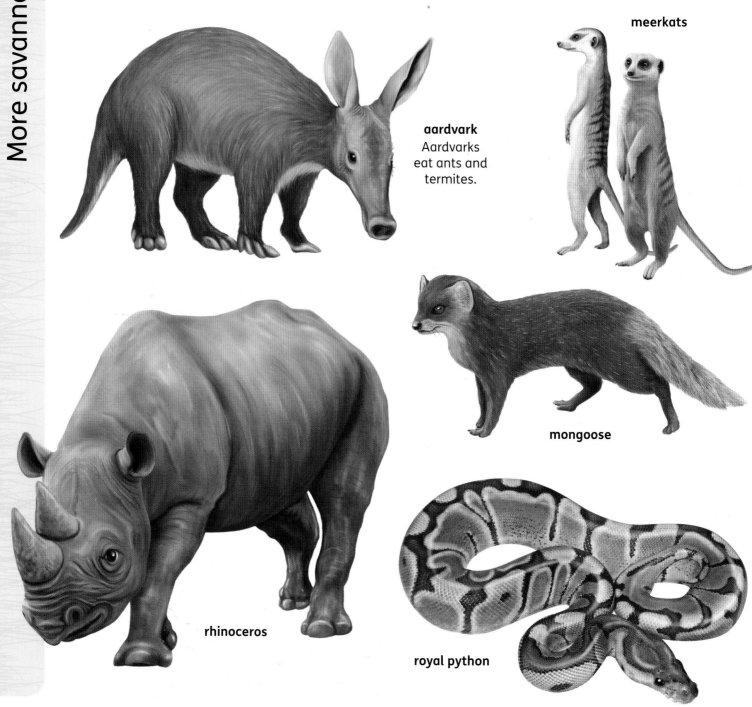

meerkats

aardvark
Aardvarks eat ants and termites.

mongoose

rhinoceros

royal python

Grassland wildlife

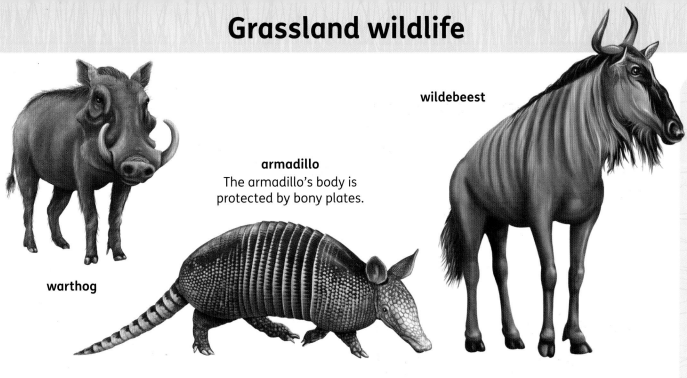

wildebeest

armadillo
The armadillo's body is
protected by bony plates.

warthog

Termite mound

Termites live in colonies with a single large
queen. They build a mound to house their queen,
and she lays eggs which will hatch to form all
the young in the colony. Some termite mounds
are as tall as a two-storey house!

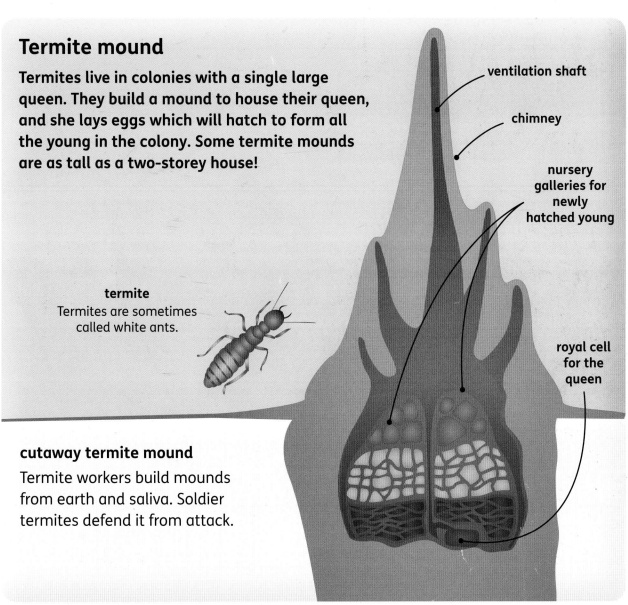

ventilation shaft

chimney

**nursery
galleries for
newly
hatched young**

**royal cell
for the
queen**

termite
Termites are sometimes
called white ants.

cutaway termite mound

Termite workers build mounds
from earth and saliva. Soldier
termites defend it from attack.

Grassland and moorland wildlife

Grassland and moorland animals are usually very well camouflaged.
This helps to keep them safe from attack. Some moorland birds, such as
grouse and partridges, fly close to the ground using bushes as cover.

emperor moth

guinea fowl

coyote
Coyotes live on the North
American prairies.

red grouse

Grassland wildlife

skylark

kestrel

hare

grasshopper

partridge

prairie dog
The prairie dog is
a kind of ground
squirrel.

ferret

Grassland wildlife

In the bush

In the Australian bush, there are rough grasses, scrubby bushes and scattered eucalyptus trees. The bush is home to many creatures that are not found anywhere else in the world. Some of these creatures are marsupials (animals that carry their young in a pouch).

1 red kangaroo

2 dingo

5 wallaby
Wallabies look like small kangaroos.

6 galah

3 blue-tongued skink

4 spiny anteater

64

7 bilby

8 emu
Emus cannot fly but they can run very fast.

9 cockatoo

10 bandicoot

11 budgerigar

12 koala

Alligators lurk in shady swamps, waiting to snap at their prey. The waters and shores of the swamps are teeming with hidden creatures...

Water habitats

Rivers, lakes, ponds and wetlands provide a range of habitats for water-dwelling creatures. They are also home to land-dwelling animals that live on the water's edge. Some species can only be found in a certain type of habitat, such as a mangrove swamp. Others live in a range of watery habitats.

Rivers and riverbanks

muskrat

hippopotamus

rainbow trout

Lakes and ponds

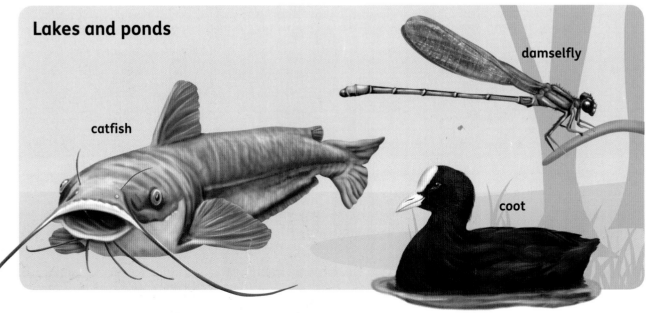

damselfly

catfish

coot

River, lake and wetland wildlife

Major rivers

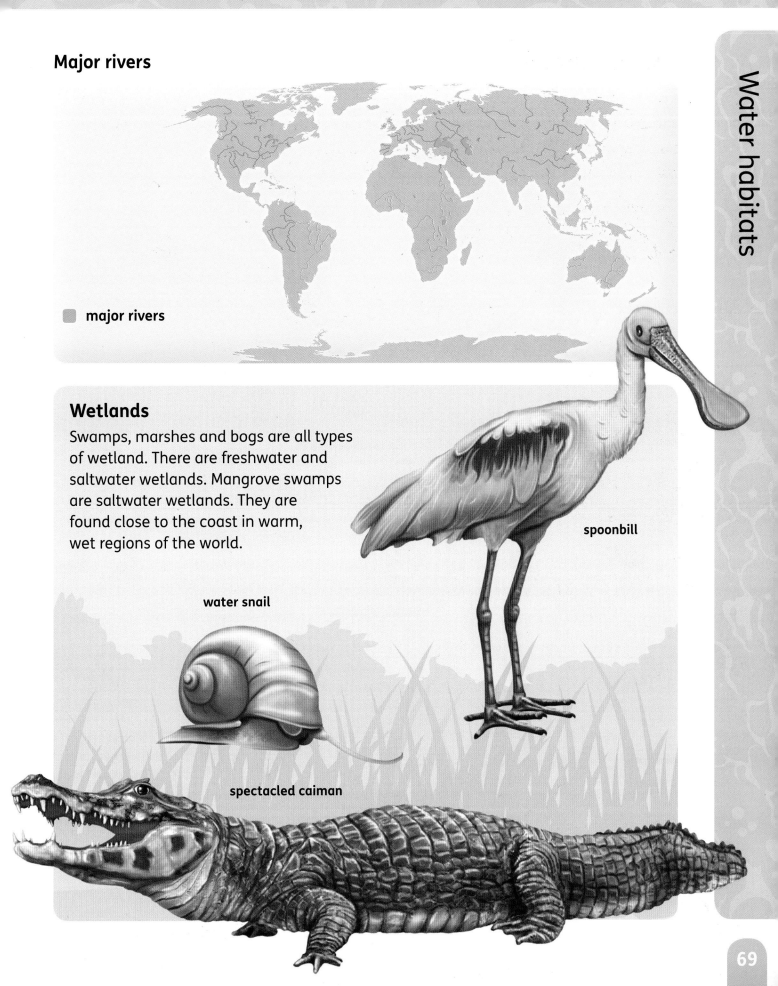

major rivers

Wetlands

Swamps, marshes and bogs are all types of wetland. There are freshwater and saltwater wetlands. Mangrove swamps are saltwater wetlands. They are found close to the coast in warm, wet regions of the world.

spoonbill

water snail

spectacled caiman

River, lake and wetland wildlife

River creatures

Rivers can be warm or icy, shallow or deep, fast or slow-moving. They also change their character, starting as a small, fast-flowing stream, and ending in a wide, shallow estuary. Each type of river is home to a different range of wildlife.

crayfish

pike

mink

anaconda
Anacondas live near rivers in the rainforest.

neon tetra
Neon tetras live in the Amazon River, but are often kept in an aquarium.

crocodile

River, lake and wetland wildlife

coypu

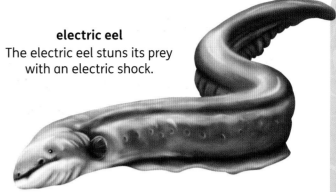

electric eel
The electric eel stuns its prey
with an electric shock.

piranha
Piranhas use their very sharp teeth
to strip the flesh off other creatures.

platypus
The platypus is a mammal that lays
eggs. It is only found in Australia.

Beaver lodge

**Beavers have a large, flat tail that they use to help them swim.
They gather twigs to build a home called a lodge.**

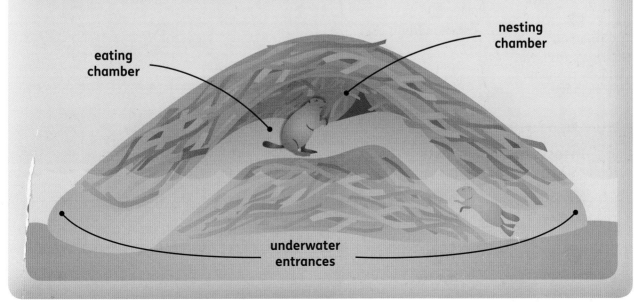

eating
chamber

nesting
chamber

underwater
entrances

Life on the river

Rivers provide a habitat for many creatures. Mammals live in burrows in the river bank. Ducks and swans glide over the water's surface, and birds catch fish and insects. Some insects fly very close to the water and some even walk on its surface!

1 heron

2 dipper
Dippers feed on insects.

3 water vole

4 water shrew

5 moorhen

6 swan

7 kingfisher
Kingfishers dive underwater to catch fish.

8 otter

9 mallard
Male mallards have brightly coloured plumage.

10 common frog

Insects and minibeasts

11 pondskater

12 dragonfly

13 greater water boatman

14 mayfly

Lake and pond wildlife

Most lakes and ponds are freshwater environments, although there are a few saltwater lakes. Few creatures live around salt lakes because these habitats provide little food or shelter.

snapping turtle

American bullfrog

pelican

common toad
Toads are often found close to ponds.

capybara

flamingo

River, lake and wetland wildlife

basilisk lizard
Basilisk lizards can run on
the surface of water.

osprey

minnow

newt

Carp

The common carp is found
in lakes. Goldfish and koi are
domesticated species of carp.
There are many different varieties
of goldfish and koi.

**common
carp**

goldfish

koi

Wetland animals

Regions that are often flooded and waterlogged are known as wetlands. They include swamps, bogs, marshes, fens, reed beds and the land around river estuaries. A swamp is a wetland region with trees. Other types of wetland have very few trees.

ibis

crane

lungfish
Lungfish have lungs as well as gills so they can breathe air during a dry season.

alligator

River, lake and wetland wildlife

diamondback terrapin

stork

Big cats of the swamp

Some big cats live in mangrove swamps, but they are in danger of becoming extinct because of poaching. Today, there are fewer than 200 Florida panthers in the wild.

Florida panther

Bengal tiger

In the desert, sand dunes stretch for miles.
Scorpions, lizards and snakes bask in the baking sun...

Desert habitats

Deserts are vast regions of arid land with almost no rainfall. Some are hot and sandy. Others are cold and rocky. The world's largest hot desert is the Sahara in North Africa. The Atacama Desert in South America is a cold desert. It is one of the driest regions on Earth.

Hot deserts

Hot deserts have scorching days and cold nights. Powerful winds race over the dunes and whip up sandstorms. There are very few plants, except at an oasis. A water pool in a desert is called an oasis.

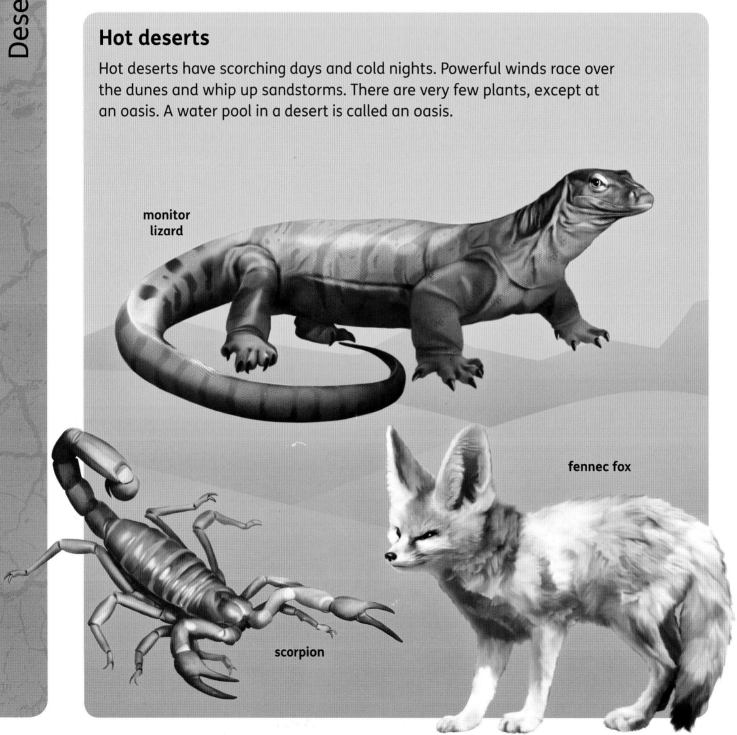

monitor lizard

scorpion

fennec fox

Main desert regions

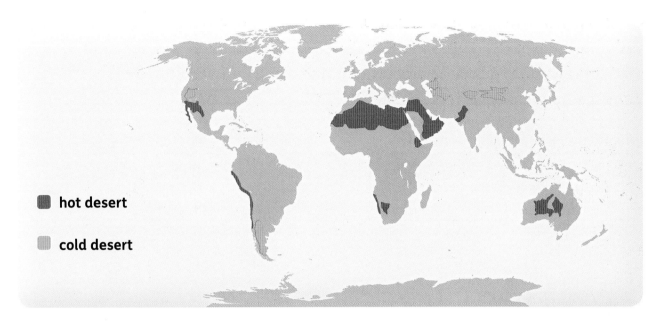

- ■ hot desert
- ▢ cold desert

Cold deserts

Cold deserts can be warm during the day, but temperatures at night drop well below freezing point. Cactus plants often grow in cold deserts.

desert tortoise

Bactrian camel

sidewinder rattlesnake

Desert creatures

Desert animals have to survive in a very harsh environment with almost no water. Some are able to store liquid in their bodies. Some burrow under the sand to keep cool. Many desert mammals are nocturnal. They only come out at night when it is cooler.

kangaroo rat

gerbil
Gerbils are sometimes kept as pets.

honeypot ant

locust

dromedary camel

Desert wildlife

black widow spider

turkey vulture
Vultures feed on the flesh of dead animals, known as carrion.

jerboa
The enormous ears of the jerboa allow it to lose body heat rapidly.

horned desert viper

roadrunner

inland taipan
The inland taipan is one of the world's most venomous snakes.

83

In the depths of the ocean, giant manta rays glide slowly and silently...

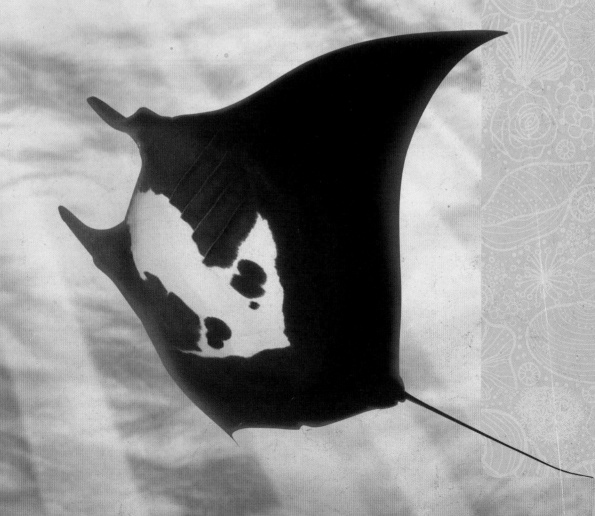

Life in the ocean

Oceans

More than two-thirds of the Earth's surface is covered by water. There are five oceans and several seas and they are home to a vast range of creatures. Creatures that live in the oceans include mammals, such as whales and dolphins, fish of all sizes, crustaceans, like lobsters and shrimps, and very simple life forms, such as tube worms.

Ocean zones

Oceans and seas can be divided into five different zones. Each zone has its own particular wildlife, but some creatures move between different zones.

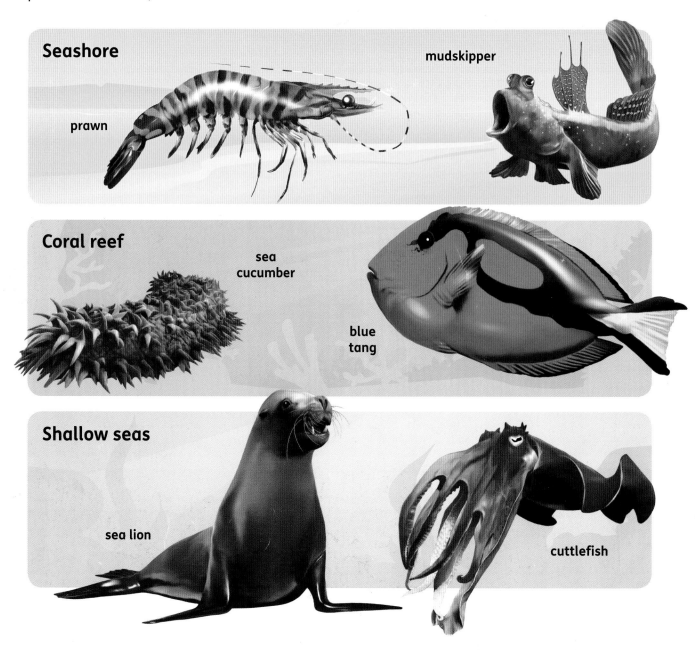

Seashore

prawn

mudskipper

Coral reef

sea cucumber

blue tang

Shallow seas

sea lion

cuttlefish

Life in the ocean

Major oceans and seas

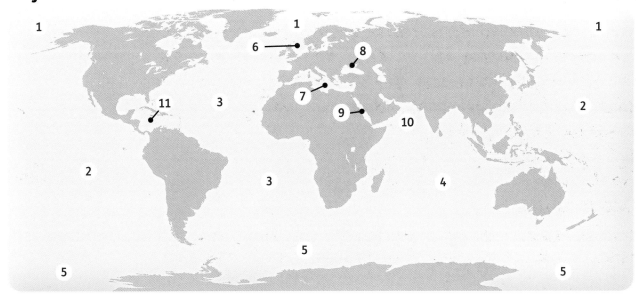

1	Arctic Ocean	5	Southern Ocean	9	Red Sea
2	Pacific Ocean	6	North Sea	10	Arabian Sea
3	Atlantic Ocean	7	Mediterranean Sea	11	Caribbean Sea
4	Indian Ocean	8	Black Sea		

Open ocean

herring

flying
fish

Deep seas

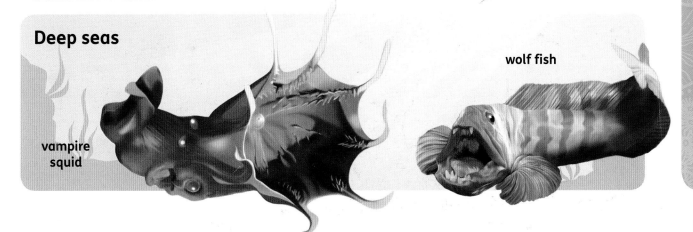

wolf fish

vampire
squid

87

On the seashore

Seashore creatures live on sand and rocks that are covered by the sea each time the tide comes in. Rock pools are home to many colourful creatures and seabirds fly along the shore looking for food.

1 oystercatcher

2 cormorant

3 crab
Crabs scuttle sideways across the sand.

4 shrimp

5 starfish

6 sea urchin

7 mussels
Mussels and barnacles feed on microscopic plankton in the water.

8 sea anemone
Sea anenomes open up under water.

9 hermit crab

10 limpets

11 barnacles

12 puffin

13 seagull

Life in the ocean

In the ocean

Thousands of species of fish live in the oceans. Smaller fish usually swim in groups, called shoals, while larger fish hunt alone. The fish on these two pages are shown roughly to scale.

1 sardine		**4** pilot fish		**7** halibut	
2 mackerel		**5** flounder		**8** sole	
3 plaice		**6** barracuda		**9** dogfish	

Life in the ocean

10 monkfish

11 sea bass

12 marlin

13 cod

14 haddock

15 tuna

16 swordfish

More ocean life

The ocean is home to some very large creatures. Whales, dolphins, porpoises, manatees and dugongs are all mammals. Sharks and rays are fish. Sea mammals like whales need air to breathe. They swim up to the surface to blow out used air and breathe in fresh air.

dolphin
Dolphins use sounds, such as clicks and whistles, to communicate with each other.

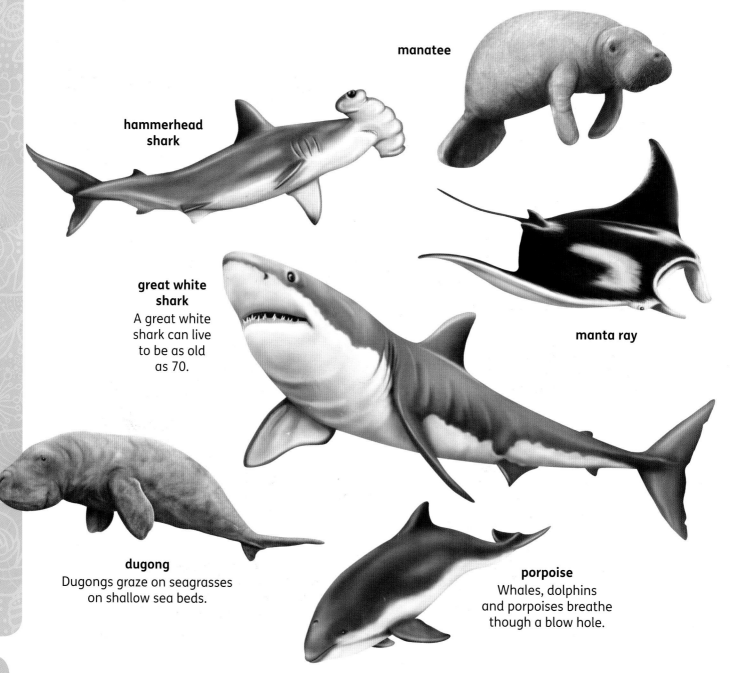

manatee

hammerhead shark

great white shark
A great white shark can live to be as old as 70.

manta ray

dugong
Dugongs graze on seagrasses on shallow sea beds.

porpoise
Whales, dolphins and porpoises breathe though a blow hole.

Life in the ocean

Whales

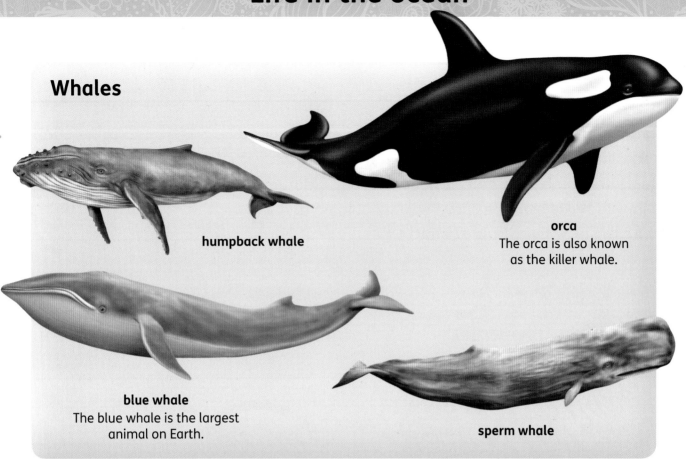

humpback whale

orca
The orca is also known
as the killer whale.

blue whale
The blue whale is the largest
animal on Earth.

sperm whale

Baleen whales

Some whales have flexible bristles called baleen inside their mouths
to help them feed. The baleen plates trap tiny sea creatures, such as
plankton and krill. When a whale raises its tongue the plankton and krill
are trapped inside its mouth.

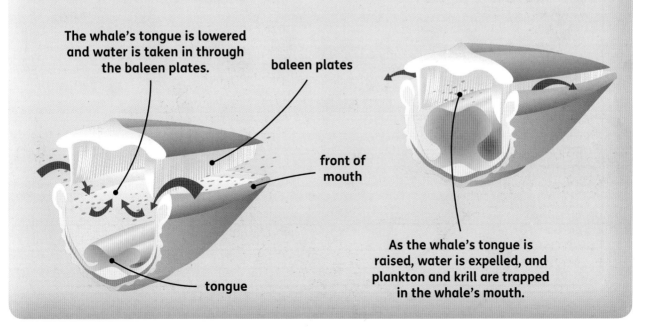

The whale's tongue is lowered
and water is taken in through
the baleen plates.

baleen plates

front of
mouth

tongue

As the whale's tongue is
raised, water is expelled, and
plankton and krill are trapped
in the whale's mouth.

Coral reefs

Coral reefs are made from living creatures! Coral polyps grow a hard outer case. When the coral dies, the casing remains and gradually builds up to form a reef. Coral reefs are home to millions of species of sea creatures. Many of these creatures have brilliant colours to blend in with the brightly coloured corals.

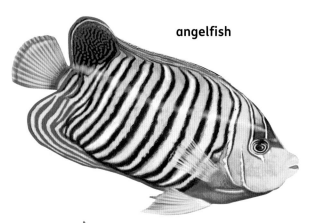

angelfish

cowry
The cowry is a species of sea snail.

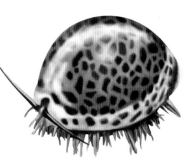

seahorse
The male seahorse carries its young in a pouch.

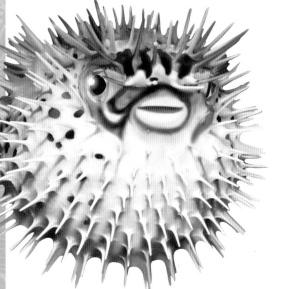

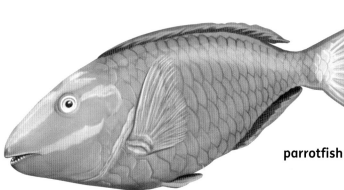

parrotfish

puffer fish
When it is threatened, the puffer fish expands by swallowing water.

giant clam

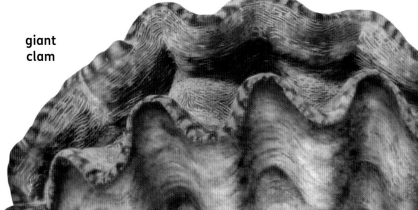

Life in the ocean

clown
fish

green turtle

triggerfish

butterfly fish

damselfish

sea pen
Sea pens feed
on plankton.

brittle star

sea goldie

lion fish

Creatures of the deep

It is almost completely dark on the ocean bed, but some deep-sea creatures can create their own light. Others have very large eyes to help them see. Sea sponges and tube worms stand on the sea bed. They are very simple creatures that look like plants.

1 hatchetfish		**4** angler fish	
2 vent fish		**5** giant tube worms	
3 lantern fish		**6** deep-sea sponges	

Life in the ocean

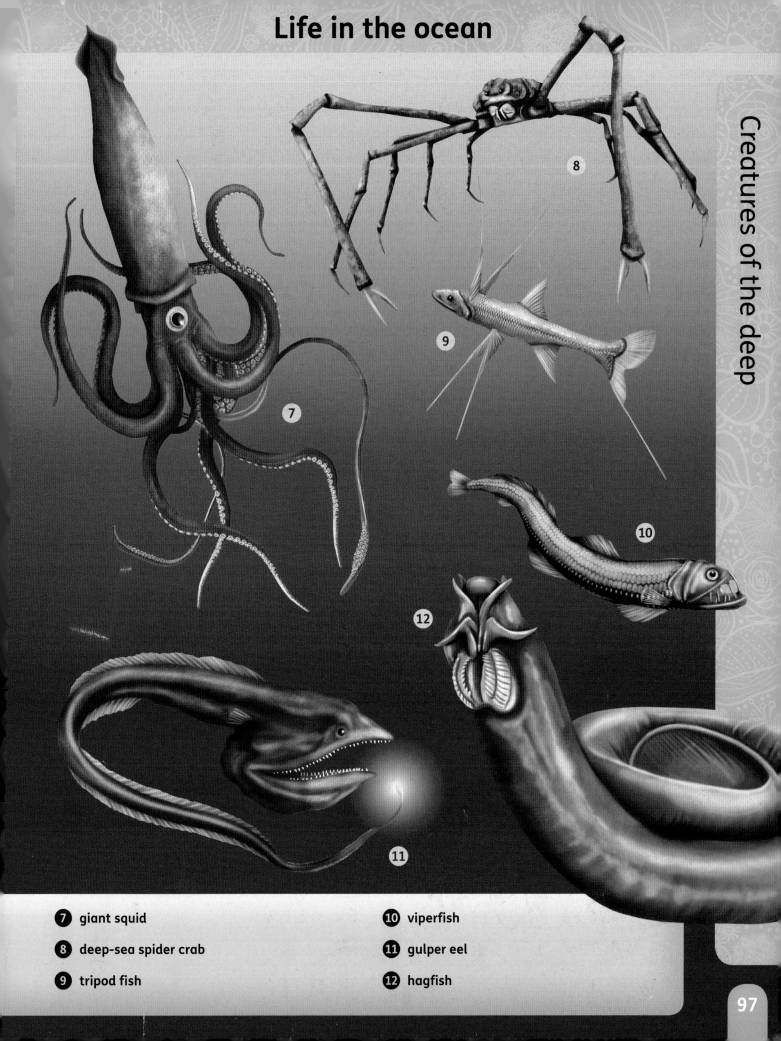

7 giant squid

8 deep-sea spider crab

9 tripod fish

10 viperfish

11 gulper eel

12 hagfish

On the Arctic ice-cap, polar bears go hunting for seals. Gulls circle overhead and whales, seals and walruses swim in the icy seas...

ANIMALS OF THE POLAR REGIONS

Animals of the polar regions

Polar habitats

The Arctic and Antarctic regions are mostly ice and rock, and only a few species of animals can survive there. They are specially adapted to the low temperatures. At the edge of the ice are freezing seas and semi-frozen land, known as tundra.

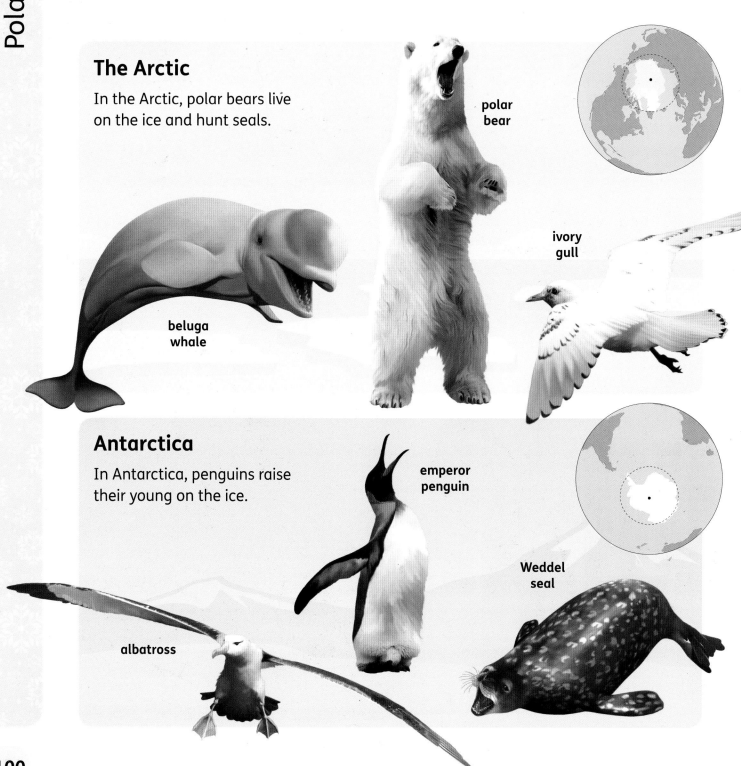

The Arctic

In the Arctic, polar bears live on the ice and hunt seals.

polar bear

beluga whale

ivory gull

Antarctica

In Antarctica, penguins raise their young on the ice.

emperor penguin

Weddel seal

albatross

Animals of the polar regions

The polar regions

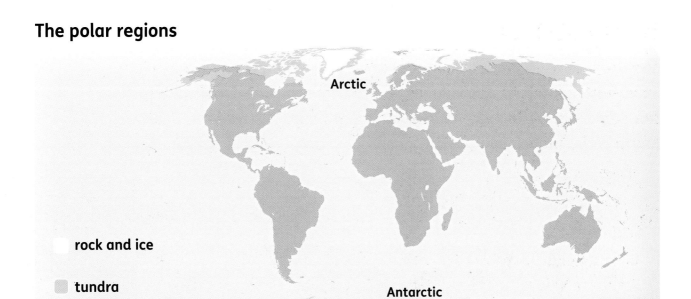

Arctic

rock and ice

tundra

Antarctic

Tundra regions

The tundra regions are covered in snow for the most of the year.

Arctic wolf

Canada goose

ermine

Arctic and Antarctic wildlife

Arctic and Antarctic wildlife

Seals are found in the Arctic and in Antarctica. Whales, fish and other sea creatures swim in the icy seas and birds fly overhead looking for food. Several species of penguins live in Antarctica but no penguins are found in the Arctic regions. The polar bear is only found in the Arctic.

Arctic skua

walrus

ringed seal
Seals are protected from the cold by a thick layer of fat known as blubber.

rockhopper penguin

Arctic skate

Animals of the polar regions

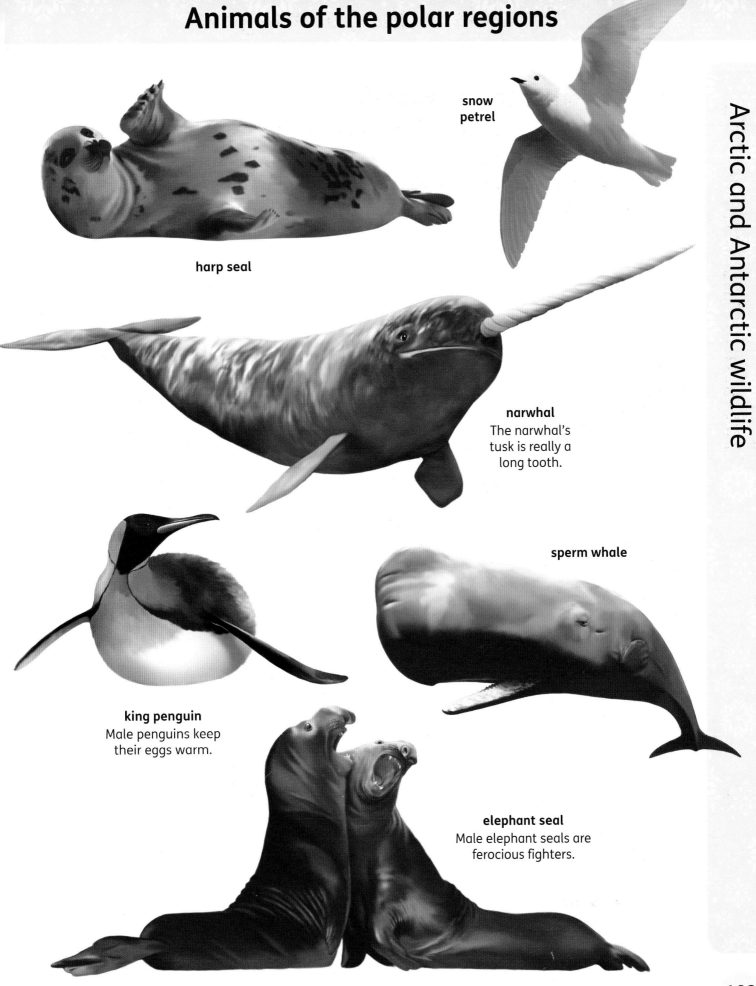

snow
petrel

harp seal

narwhal
The narwhal's
tusk is really a
long tooth.

sperm whale

king penguin
Male penguins keep
their eggs warm.

elephant seal
Male elephant seals are
ferocious fighters.

Life in the tundra

Tundra regions have very short summers. In these warmer months, the snow disappears and the icy ground becomes soft. Some animals shed their winter coats and some emerge from burrows where they have sheltered.

Arctic hare

caribou
Caribou are also known as reindeer.

snow goose

eider duck
Eider ducks have very soft feathers called down that they use to line their nests.

Arctic lemming

Animals of the polar regions

grizzly
bear

Snowy owl

Adaptations to snow

Arctic fox

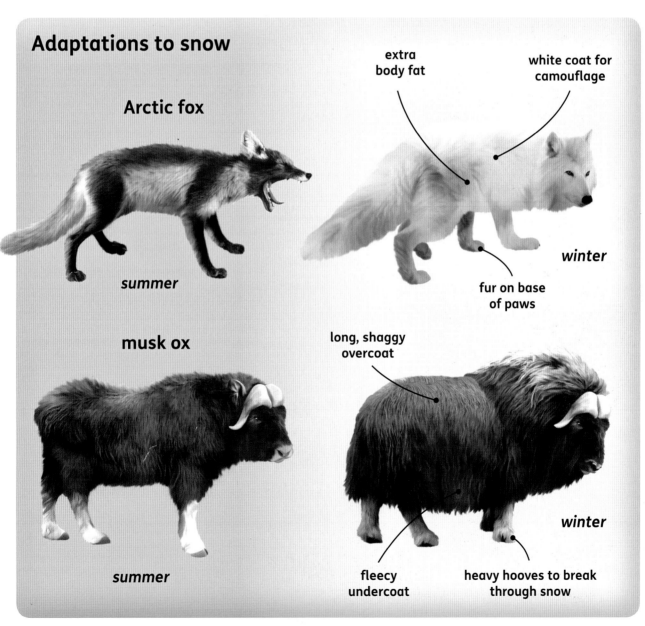

extra
body fat

white coat for
camouflage

summer

fur on base
of paws

winter

musk ox

long, shaggy
overcoat

summer

fleecy
undercoat

heavy hooves to break
through snow

winter

Widespread creatures

Some animals are found in a wide range of habitats across the world. These widespread creatures include many species of insects and minibeasts. Insects often live on food or plants, and this means they are easily transported around the world.

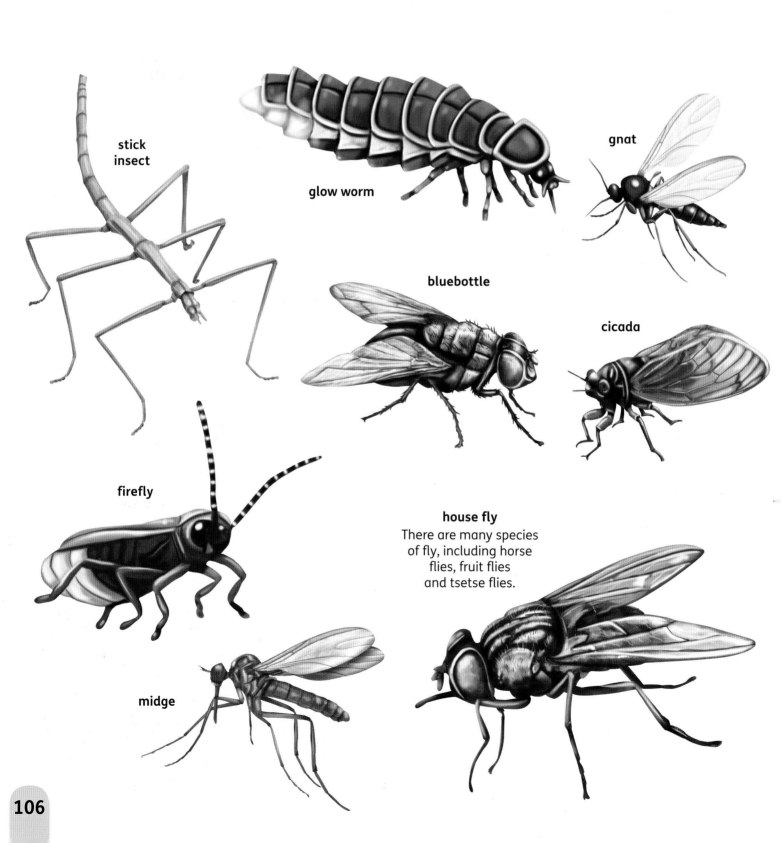

stick insect

glow worm

gnat

bluebottle

cicada

firefly

house fly
There are many species of fly, including horse flies, fruit flies and tsetse flies.

midge

Widespread creatures

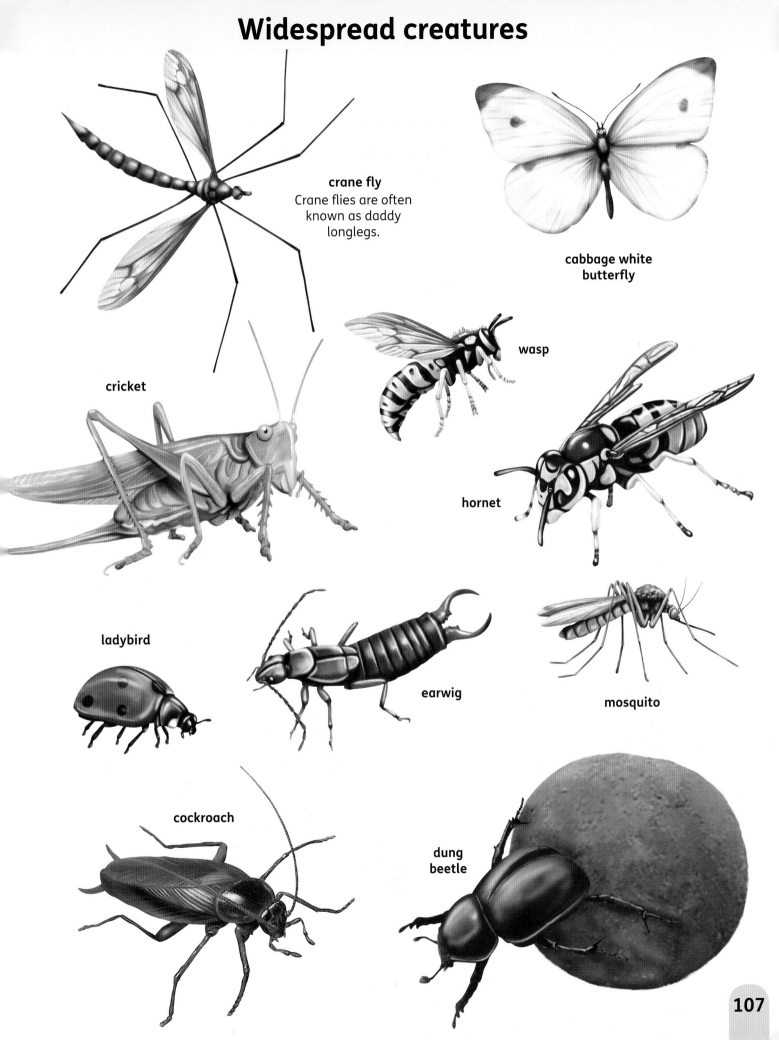

crane fly
Crane flies are often known as daddy longlegs.

cabbage white butterfly

wasp

cricket

hornet

ladybird

earwig

mosquito

cockroach

dung beetle

Widespread birds

Some types of bird are found in many parts of the world. Here are some common examples. (Birds in different countries sometimes have the same name but do not belong to the same species.
The robin and the blackbird are examples of this.)

jackdaw
Jackdaws belong to the crow family.

cuckoo

chaffinch
The chaffinch belongs to the finch family. Other finches include the bullfinch and the goldfinch.

thrush

Peacock
Peacocks are domesticated in many parts of the world. They live in the wild in Africa and Asia.

Widespread birds

skylark

sparrow

starling

blackbird

swan
Australian swans are black.

wren

collared dove

pigeon
Pigeons are found in large numbers in cities.

magpie

What do you call a baby animal?

ANIMAL	YOUNG
antelope	*calf*
badger	*cub*
bear	*cub*
beaver	*kit*
bobcat	*kitten*
buffalo	*calf*
camel	*calf*
caribou	*fawn*
cougar	*kitten*
coyote	*puppy*
dog	*puppy / pup / whelp*

ANIMAL	YOUNG
eagle	*eaglet*
eel	*elver*
elephant	*calf*
ferret	*kit*
fish	*fry*
frog	*tadpole*
giraffe	*calf*
goose	*gosling*
hare	*leveret*
horse	*foal / colt (male) / filly (female)*

Vocabulary builder

ANIMAL	YOUNG	ANIMAL	YOUNG
kangaroo	*joey*	swan	*cygnet*
lion	*cub*	tiger	*cub*
owl	*owlet*	toad	*tadpole*
pigeon	*squab / squeaker*	wallaby	*joey*
pike	*pickerel*	walrus	*cub*
rhinoceros	*calf*	weasel	*kit*
salmon	*parr / smolt*	whale	*calf*
seal	*calf / pup*	wolf	*cub / pup / whelp*
spider	*spiderling*	zebra	*foal*

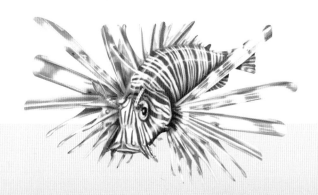

What do you call a group of...?

ants	*a colony*
bees	*a swarm*
birds	*a flock*
dolphins	*a school*
fish	*a shoal / a school*
geese	*a gaggle / a flock*
lions	*a pride*
monkeys	*a troop*
whales	*a pod*
wolves	*a pack*

Vocabulary builder

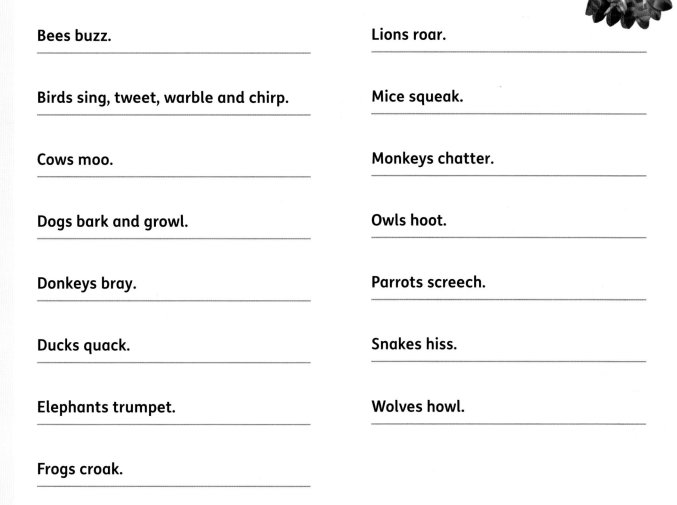

What noise does an animal make?

Bees buzz.

Birds sing, tweet, warble and chirp.

Cows moo.

Dogs bark and growl.

Donkeys bray.

Ducks quack.

Elephants trumpet.

Frogs croak.

Hens cluck.

Horses neigh and whinny.

Lions roar.

Mice squeak.

Monkeys chatter.

Owls hoot.

Parrots screech.

Snakes hiss.

Wolves howl.

Animal word origins

Some animal names have interesting origins. They come from different languages, perhaps from the way the animal looks, like 'rhinoceros', or the noise that it makes, such as 'cuckoo'. The technical name for the study of word origins is 'etymology'. Here are the origins of some of the names of animals you can find in this book.

aardvark is from Afrikaans, from *aarde* meaning 'earth' and *vark* meaning 'pig'

alligator is from Spanish, from *el lagarto* meaning 'the lizard'

anemone is from a Greek word meaning 'windflower' (from the belief that the flower opens when it is windy)

animal is from Latin *animalis* meaning 'having breath'

antelope is from a late Greek word *antholops* (which was originally the name of a mythical creature)

armadillo is from Spanish *armado* meaning 'armed man'

badger is perhaps from 'badge', because of the markings on a badger's head. The word dates from the 16th century; the earlier Old English word for a badger was 'brock'.

barnacle first referred to a kind of goose which was once believed to hatch from shellfish attached to rocks

basilisk is from Greek *basilikos* which originally meant 'little king' and is related to our words 'basil' and 'basilica'

beaver is from an Old English word *beetle* which is from Old English *bitula*, from bitan 'to bite', because of its biting mouthparts

Vocabulary builder

budgerigar is from Australian Aboriginal *budgeri* meaning 'good' and *gar* meaning 'cockatoo'

buzzard is from Latin *buteo* meaning 'falcon'

caterpillar is from Old French *chatepelose* meaning 'hairy cat'

centipede is from *centi-* and a Latin word *pedes* meaning 'feet'

crocodile is from a Greek word *krokodilos* meaning 'worm of the stones'

cuckoo is named after the sound of its call

dromedary camel is from Greek *dromas* meaning 'runner'

ferret is from Latin *fur* meaning 'thief'

flamingo is from a Spanish word *flamengo*, and is connected to the Latin *flamma* meaning 'a flame' because of its colour

gorilla is from a Greek word, which is probably from an African word denoting a wild or hairy person

halibut is from 'holy' and *butt*, a dialect word meaning 'flatfish' (because it was eaten on Christian holy days, when meat was forbidden)

hippopotamus is from Greek *hippos* meaning 'horse' and *potamos* meaning 'river'

kangaroo is an Australian Aboriginal word

lobster is via Old English from a Latin word *locusta* meaning 'crustacean' or 'locust'

Vocabulary builder

penguin is possibly from Welsh *pen gwyn* meaning 'white head'

piranha comes via Portuguese from Tupi (a South American language)

plaice is from Greek *platys* meaning 'broad'

porcupine is from Old French *porc espin* meaning 'spiny pig'

porpoise is from the Latin words *porcus* meaning 'pig' and *piscis* meaning 'python' which is from Python, the name of a huge serpent killed by Apollo in Greek legend

reptile is from Latin *reptilis* meaning 'crawling'

rhinoceros is from Greek *rhinos* meaning 'of the nose' and *keras* meaning 'horn'

snake is from an Old English word *snaca* meaning 'to crawl' or 'to creep'

spider is from an Old English word *spithra* meaning 'spinner'

springbok is an Afrikaans word, from Dutch *springen* meaning 'to spring' and *bok* meaning 'buck' or 'antelope'

squirrel is from Greek *skiouros* which is from *skia* meaning 'shadow' and *oura* meaning 'tail' (because its long bushy tail cast a shadow over its body and kept it cool)

tadpole is from toad and an old word *poll* meaning 'head'

tarantula is from Taranto in southern Italy, because the spider's bite was thought to cause tarantism, a psychological illness once common in southern Italy

wildebeest is an Afrikaans word meaning 'wild beast'

Animal idioms

An idiom is a phrase or group of words that have a special meaning that is not obvious from the words themselves, for example, 'to be in hot water' means to be in trouble or difficulty. Here are some idioms which feature some of the animals in this book.

a busy bee
a very busy person

keep the wolf from the door
to avoid going hungry

on a wild goose chase
To be on a wild goose chase is to be searching for something that is impossible to find, so that you waste a lot of time.

like a fish out of water
If you are like a fish out of water, you feel awkward because you are in a situation that is not at all familiar.

have a bee in your bonnet
If you have a bee in your bonnet about something, you cannot stop thinking or talking about it because you think it is very important.

it's the bee's knees
If you think something is really excellent, you can say 'it's the bees knees'.

hold your horses
wait a moment, don't be so hasty

a leopard can't change its spots
people can't change their basic nature

put the cart before the horse
to do things in the wrong order

straight from the horse's mouth
Information that is straight from the horse's mouth is from the person who is most directly involved and so is likely to be accurate. It is as if a horse in a horse race was telling you which horse was going to win the race.

the straw that broke the camel's back
a small difficulty that, coming on top of a lot of other difficulties, makes a situation too much to bear

Animal detective quiz

How much do you know about animals?

Try this animal detective quiz and track down the creatures in the pages of this book. The answers are at the back of the book.

Animal hunters

1. Which creature injects its victims with deadly saliva?

2. Which creature sucks blood from larger animals?

3. Which creature stuns its prey with an electric shock ?

Watch out!

4. Which animal warns off attackers by producing a very strong smell?

5. Which animal warns off attackers by swallowing water to make itself look larger?

6. Which animal warns off attackers by displaying warning colours to show it is poisonous?

Special features

7. Which creature has bony plates covering its body?

8. Which creature has enormous ears that can lose heat fast?

9. Which creature has a long tongue for sucking nectar?

Animal detective quiz

Unusual behaviour

10. Which animal can run on the surface of water?

11. Which animal communicates by using clicks and whistles?

12. Which animal sleeps for around 20 hours a day?

Animal homes

13. Which creature lives in a lodge?

14. Which creature builds a home from earth and saliva?

15. Which creature lives inside the guts of other animals?

Animal parts

16. Which animal has a spinneret?

17. Which animal has a dewlap?

18. Which animal has a siphon?

What am I?

19. I am a mammal that lays eggs.

20. I am a fish that can breathe on land.

Index

Index

Index

Index

Index

Index

Quiz answers

Animal hunters

1. assassin bug	(p. 32)
2. leech	(pp. 10–11)
3. electric eel	(p. 71)

Watch out!

4. skunk	(p. 46)
5. puffer fish	(p. 94)
6. poison dart frog	(p. 35)

Special features

7. armadillo	(p. 61)
8. jerboa	(p. 83)
9. hummingbird	(p. 35)

Unusual behaviour

10. basilisk lizard	(p. 75)

Quiz answers

11. dolphin   (p. 92)

12. three-toed sloth   (p. 37)

Animal homes

 13. beaver   (p. 71)

14. termite   (p. 61)

15. tapeworm   (p. 10)

Animal parts

16. spider   (p. 26)

17. frog   (p. 22)

18. octopus   (p. 25)

What am I?

19. platypus   (p. 71)

20. lungfish   (p. 76)